Insider Guide

Industries and Careers for MBAs

2005 Edition

Helping you make smarter career decisions.

WetFeet, Inc.

609 Mission Street
Suite 400
San Francisco, CA 94105

Phone: (415) 284-7900 or 1-800-926-4JOB
Fax: (415) 284-7910
E-mail: info@wetfeet.com
Website: www.wetfeet.com

Industries and Careers for MBAs

ISBN: 1-58207-430-5

Introduction

The purpose of this Insider Guide is to provide you with a broad range of information about careers and industries, so that you can consider a full range of career options available to MBAs.

The guide is divided into two sections. The first section provides information about a variety of industries that hire MBAs, from biotechnology to venture capital. These industry profiles will give you an idea of what's going on in various industries, opportunities that may be available within, and companies that may be most likely to offer those opportunities. Most of these industry profiles contain descriptions of jobs specific to the industries in which MBAs might make a good fit. Be aware that, in addition to those jobs specified, just about every industry will offer opportunities in the standard corporate functions: marketing, operations, finance, and so on. The second section consists of profiles of a variety of career functions, from business development to project management, which you will find across a range of industries.

This guide is an initial resource to help you in your career management process. You can access additional information for many of the industries and careers profiled in this book by going to www.WetFeet.com. Other industries and careers are also profiled on the site. In each section, other Web-based resources are listed to help you learn more.

Good luck!

Careers 149

Table of Contents

Industries

Biotechnology and Pharmaceuticals

Industry Overview

Pharmaceutical companies produce and market drugs, from familiar over-the-counter compounds such as aspirin to exotic prescriptions that inhibit, activate, or otherwise affect individual molecules involved in specific medical conditions. They also produce livestock feed supplements, vitamins, and a host of other products. America's pharmaceutical industry is consistently one of the most profitable in the United States. The drug business is booming: Globally, the industry sells more than $300 billion worth of drugs each year.

Biotechnology is a relatively new kid on the block. Simply put, biotechnology, the applied knowledge of biology, seeks to duplicate or change the function of a living cell so it will work in a more predictable and controllable way. The biotech industry uses advances in genetics research to develop products for human diseases and conditions. Several biotech companies also use genetic technology to other ends, such as the manipulation of crops.

Biotech opportunities largely mirror those in the pharmaceutical industry. The key difference is that biotech firms are much more focused on research because they are still developing their initial products. Marketing and sales forces grow when—and if—a viable product nears FDA approval. This means that jobs for nonscientists are scarcer in biotech than in pharmaceuticals.

This is an industry with a potent and promising future. Demand for drugs is growing, fueled by an aging global population and blossoming international markets—Europe, Latin America, and especially Asia are the hot regions. The industry has maintained growth rates nearly double those of the economy at large and is expected to maintain that performance well into the next decade. But take note: Anybody with a genuine interest in pharmaceuticals or biotech should get acquainted with the details of the industry mergers that have occurred in the past decade.

Trends

Pricing

Insiders say this may be the biggest issue the industry currently faces. Who will pay the cost of drug development? As more treatments become available, will only the wealthy have access to them?

Prescription drug prices are rising annually, while insurers are getting stricter and stricter about which medications they'll reimburse their customers for. Exciting new drugs can cost thousands or even tens of thousands of dollars per treatment. Providing price relief for seniors has been an issue for several years. Many favor price controls to prevent costs from skyrocketing, a move the pharmaceutical industry opposes. And the pricing battle has gone international. In 2001, 39 pharmaceutical companies filed a lawsuit to prevent Africa from buying knock-offs of drugs that are still under patent protection. But these countries, where as much as 25 percent of the adult population is HIV-positive, can't afford to buy AIDS drugs, which cost between $900 and $6,200 per patient annually for moderate treatment. In Uganda, per capita income is $1,060; in South Africa, it's $6,900. Drug companies contend that they must protect their patents because this is the only way they can generate sufficient revenue to pay for the continued research that leads to the discovery of new medicines. After negotiations, pharma companies are now selling drugs in Africa below cost, and while this might solve one problem of access, it will put more pressure on the industry to maintain its pricing structure elsewhere in the world. Indeed, drugs sold at lower prices in Africa have already turned up for sale at higher market prices in Europe.

O, Canada

Many patients have been responding to high drug prices (many of the newer drugs on the market carry a price tag of $175 per month or more) by buying drugs from other countries. Canada's the country in the spotlight these days, as it ships more and more pharmaceuticals to patients in America. But importing prescription drugs is illegal in the United States—and, according to the Food & Drug Administration, unsafe. The pharma companies hate this trend, of course, because their profits will be hurt if people can buy drugs at cheaper prices than the drug companies want to get in the United States. To fight this trend, Pfizer, for one, is shutting off supplies to Canadian drug retailers who are exporting prescription drugs to the United States, and other big drugmakers are threatening to follow suit. A number of U.S. states, meanwhile, are gearing up to go after Big Pharma on behalf of their citizens, who, they say, should be able to buy drugs at the lower prices they can get by importing them.

Still More Ethical and Legal Concerns

The biotech and pharmaceutical industries seem to be facing wave after wave of bad press in recent times. "Green" types have been gathering evidence to support their claims that biotechnology-produced foods are unsafe, and their voice of protest has been getting louder and louder; indeed, as this guide goes to press, anti–modified-foods activists are being arrested in the streets of San Francisco as they protest outside a biotech industry conference.

Meanwhile, drug companies are also coming under fire for some of their clinical-trials practices. Many drug companies test their drugs overseas, in poor countries where it's easier and cheaper to recruit test participants. The question on the mind of critics, though, is, What do drugmakers do when their tests are over? In many cases, test participants were receiving medications that vastly improved their quality of life. Should drugmakers be able to cut off the supply of the drugs they're testing once those tests are over? Should drugmakers be obliged to provide the drugs that they've tested in poor countries in those countries once the drugs have gone to market? Companies are grappling with these and similar questions. Some have tried marketing drugs in poor countries where they've been tested, but with so few in those countries able to afford the drugs, that's a money-losing proposition.

Drugmakers are also facing criticism for in effect buying influence with state and federal government officials. For example, in early 2004, some U.S. senators called the National Institutes of Health to task for allowing its scientists to accept consulting compensation from pharma and biotech companies.

The Human Genome Map . . .

. . . may finally be yielding some bottom-line results. The interesting thing is that, so far, the benefits the pharma and biotech industry is receiving from the human genome map is not in the form of new drugs, but rather in the drug-testing process. Companies such as Merck and Millennium Pharmaceuticals are using DNA chips, or gene expression arrays, to weed out bad drugs earlier in the development process. The hope is that this technology will allow companies to cut the development cost for new drugs, which currently averages $800 million to $900 million. A bit farther down the road, companies hope to benefit from the new technology by targeting specific patient populations for whom specific drugs would work best.

Let's Make a Deal

Because the cost of soup-to-nuts drug development, manufacturing, marketing, and sales is prohibitive, a growing number of biotech companies that once dreamed of competing on equal terms with Big Pharma, the handful of multinational giants that dominate the industry, now instead seek partnerships. The nature of these alliances varies: In some instances, a biotech shop exchanges an exclusive license to market and sell a patented drug to a pharmaceutical company that is willing to pay some research costs up front. Such agreements may also include limited use of the pharmaceutical company's manufacturing and distribution channels.

In other instances, a pharmaceutical company makes a cash investment in exchange for a portion of future revenue and/or an equity stake in the biotech partner. This type of relationship is often tied to a marketing and distribution deal like the one described above. As a result, it's not unusual for Big Pharma to have biotech holdings that give them a substantial piece of the action.

How It Breaks Down

Big Pharma

Insiders refer to the handful of multinational giants that dominate the industry as Big Pharma. The majority of Big Pharma companies are headquartered in the United States, but several are based in Western Europe—Switzerland, Germany, and France. Those headquartered in the United States are all located east of the Mississippi, with the greatest concentration in New Jersey.

A wave of consolidation has engulfed this industry, with already-giant companies merging into even larger companies. One recent example is Pfizer's acquisition of Pharmacia. One driver for consolidation is that patents on a significant number of blockbuster drugs, such as Prozac and Zantac, have recently or are about to expire. When patents expire, the market is opened to competition from lower-priced generic versions of the drug. Sales can drop by as much as 80 percent, leaving drug companies scrambling to pick up the slack. While some look to consolidate resources through mergers and acquisitions, others believe that signing pacts with biotech is the best way to shore up their product pipelines.

Big Pharma companies come in two styles: diversified and nondiversified. Diversified companies—which include Johnson & Johnson, Abbott Labs, and Wyeth, maintain other health care–related businesses, such as consumer health product divisions and medical device companies, while those that are nondiversified—Eli Lilly, Merck—focus solely on the development and sale of drugs. In recent times, though, diversified companies have been choosing to divest their nonpharma concerns in favor of the leaner and more profitable drug business. Bristol-Myers Squibb, for instance, recently sold Clairol, the number-one hair-products company in the United States, to Procter & Gamble.

Biotech

Despite the success of such biotech giants as Amgen and Genentech, a large majority of biotech shops are still small enough for everyone to know everyone else's name. But a growing number of companies are joining the elite group of biotech firms that have FDA-approved drugs on the market; between 2000 and 2003, the FDA approved some 132 new drugs and vaccines and new indications for existing products. Once a biotech company has reached the stage at which it is bringing a product to market, its jobs expand from the primarily science-focused to include marketing, manufacturing, engineering, and sales. Culturally, companies tend to have growing pains as they move from R&D to commercialization, but their organizations tend to remain much leaner and flatter than those in Big Pharma.

Although there are 1,466 biotech firms in the United States (318 of them publicly traded), with some 200,000 total employees, the biotech industry is significantly smaller than the pharma industry. Still, this is a vibrant sector. Between 1992 and 2002, revenue for the industry more than tripled, from $8 billion in 1992 to nearly $30 billion in 2002. And while funding for biotech concerns dropped in the early 2000s, this remains one of the industries where investors are most likely to put their money. Indeed, according to PricewaterhouseCoopers' Money Tree survey of venture capital investments, while down from a peak of $4.25

billion in 2000, VC investment in biotech companies was still quite strong in 2003 ($3.44 billion) and on the rise (up from $2.95 billion in 2002, with first-quarter 2004 coming in at $943 million, versus $660 million in first-quarter 2003).

Biotech companies tend to be located in geographical clusters, often near prominent research universities. The largest concentration of biotech companies is in California (in and around the San Francisco Bay Area and San Diego, mainly), followed closely by Massachusetts, but you'll also find pockets in such far-flung regions as Washington, D.C.; Raleigh-Durham, North Carolina; and Boulder, Colorado.

Key Jobs for MBAs

A note about salaries: At large pharmaceutical companies, people in management positions earn significant bonuses in cash and stock options. At many biotech companies, all employees receive stock options, which, if the company does well, can be lucrative. These bonuses are not reflected in the salary ranges here.

Marketing Analyst/Associate Product Manager

Job seekers without backgrounds in science can find work on the marketing side in Big Pharma and large biotech companies. A marketing analyst is primarily responsible for coordinating and implementing campaigns for specific drugs and/or audiences. Many MBAs enter the industry this way, and—perhaps more important—few without MBAs move far beyond the marketing analyst level, although this varies from company to company.

Salary range: $38,000 to $75,000.

Product Manager

This job requires managing a team of people and working to determine price, distribution, brand image, forecasting, and overall strategy for one or more drugs. On a micro level, the job can be claustrophobic—imagine spending 13 months of 6-day weeks learning every aspect of a single drug, and then having the company decide that it would be best simply to let the product die. But over the years you should be exposed to some of the most important, dynamic, and profitable drug markets in the industry—an experience that will give you a synoptic overview and make you a greater asset to the company.

Salary range: $60,000 to $100,000.

Job Prospects

According to the Bureau of Labor Statistics, employment in the biotech and pharmaceutical industries will increase at a faster rate than the average through 2010.

While Big Pharma controls most action in the industry, you can opt to work in some of the more specialized areas of biotechnology, where companies range in size from a handful of employees to several thousand.

Biotech offers a rich array of job prospects. People with all sorts of backgrounds find careers here—not only the scientists you'd expect, but also engineers, businesspeople, computer programmers, and health care professionals. There is also a growing need in specialized projects for nutritionists, environmentalists, and law enforcement specialists, among others.

The burn rate—the steep cost of research for the many products that don't make it to market—always affects who gets hired and when, so it's important to review this aspect of your potential employers' financials as thoroughly as possible.

Big Pharma companies are good places to work if you like stability. Many people will spend whole careers at a single company, enjoying the traditional accoutrements of corporate life, including generous annual stock-option grants for managers.

Key Biotech and Pharmaceutical Companies by 2003 Revenue			
Company	Revenue ($M)	1-Yr. Change (%)	Employees
Pfizer	45,188	40	122,000
Johnson & Johnson	41,862	15	110,600
GlaxoSmithKline	38,238	12	106,166
Roche Group	25,132	17	65,357
Novartis	24,864	7	78,541
Merck	22,486	−57	30,828
Aventis	22,397	3	75,000
Bristol-Myers Squibb	20,894	15	44,000
Abbot Laboratories	19,681	11	72,200
AstraZeneca	18,849	6	60,000
Wyeth	15,851	9	52,385
Eli Lilly	12,583	14	46,100
Amgen	8,356	51	12,900
Schering-Plough	8,334	−18	30,500
GE Healthcare Bio-Sciences	2,800	13	10,051
Genentech	2,799	24	6,226
Forest Laboratories	2,650*	20	4,240
Serono	1,858	20	4,597
Allergan	1,771	24	4,930
Chiron Corp.	1,766	82	5,332

*2004 numbers.
Sources: Hoover's; WetFeet analysis.

Additional Resources

Bio.com (www.bio.com)

BioView (www.bioview.com)

InPharm.com (www.inpharm.com)

Knowledge @ Wharton: Health Economics
(knowledge.wharton.upenn.edu/category.cfm?catid=6)

McKinsey Quarterly: Health Care
(www.mckinseyquarterly.com/category_editor.asp?L2=12)

Pharmaceutical Online (www.pharmaceuticalonline.com)

Commercial Banking

Industry Overview

Asked why he robbed banks, Willie Sutton replied, "Because that's where the money is." That was in the '30s, but even today, despite changes, a lot of the money is still in commercial banks. Most of us maintain checking accounts at commercial banks and use their ATMs. The money we deposit in our neighborhood bank branch or credit union supports local economic activity through small business loans, mortgages, auto loans, and home repair loans. The bank also provides loans in the form of credit card charges, and it renders local services including safe deposit, notary, and merchant banking. The bank branch or credit union office remains the cornerstone of Main Street economic life.

But that doesn't mean the industry isn't changing. Traditionally a staid business (think: gray suits and conversations conducted in hushed voices and formal tones), banking is now entering a whole new world. For one thing, there's the move of banking onto the Web, where companies such as Bank of America now conduct much of their banking business with customers. For another, there's the explosion in branch banking, as banks like Washington Mutual attempt to become as ubiquitous as 7-Eleven stores in the American landscape. And thanks to the repeal of the Glass-Steagall Act, which limited the businesses commercial banks could operate in, there's the move among banks into nontraditional businesses such as insurance products and securities.

Trends

Consolidation and New Jobs

For decades, banks profited by simply holding customers' money and charging them check-writing fees and interest on loans. Jobs were well defined and stable, and the paths to promotion were clear and secure. Not anymore. Consolidation, competition, and technological change are shaking the industry to its core, forcing layoffs while creating opportunity.

Since 1995, more than 200 large and small banks have merged. A handful of recently consolidated giants—Citigroup, Bank of America, J.P. Morgan Chase, Bank One—dominate the banking industry. The new behemoths are entering new markets, while replacing service personnel with online and other technologies. However, hiring by a growing number of nonbanks compensates for this trend to a degree. These firms, which are pioneering new ways of delivering financial services, include MBNA and Capital One, which are credit card lenders, and transaction processing and data services providers such as First Data and Fiserv.

Deregulation

The Glass-Steagall Act, passed by Congress in 1933, served as the backbone of banking regulation. During the late '90s, however, banks and other financial institutions found ways around the restrictions placed on them by Glass-Steagall and related legislation. Finally, in late 1999, Glass-Steagall was repealed, eliminating the legal framework for Depression-era boundaries for financial services firms. The big firms were already skirting the Glass-Steagall boundaries—for instance, Citigroup could offer customers insurance through its Travelers subsidiary—when Glass-Steagall was overturned in 1999. But now even smaller players in commercial banking can offer everything from insurance to securities products.

Problem Loans and Lower Profits

Just so you know that it's not all sweetness and light in the commercial banking industry: Bankruptcies at companies such as Enron and Kmart and the fact that most companies have been so concerned with cutting costs that they haven't given much thought to purchasing new equipment or building new facilities, combined with other factors, have caused an ongoing slump in commercial lending.

On the consumer side of the business, 2003 saw the largest number of individual bankruptcies in U.S. history, meaning underperforming loans for banks. And the mortgage-lending boom seems to have come to an end; indeed, some project mortgage lending will be cut in half throughout this year.

How It Breaks Down

As a job seeker, the most important distinction to keep in mind is between regional banks and the big global ones. Here we've broken down the industry by type of banking, rather than size of player, since banks are increasingly adding new services to their array of traditional ones.

Consumer or Retail Banking

This is what most people think of when they think of banking: a small to midsized branch with tellers and platform officers—the men and women in suits sitting at the nice wooden desks with pen sets—to handle customers' day-to-day needs. Although thousands of small community banks, credit unions, and savings institutions still exist, employment opportunities are increasingly coming from a few mega-players such as Citibank, Bank of America, and Bank One, most of which seem hell-bent on building national—and even international—banking operations.

One complicating factor in this picture is that the banks mentioned above, in addition to extending their consumer-banking operations, have added to their portfolios by strengthening their investment-banking and asset management capabilities, among others. So, if you want to work at a Citibank branch, make sure that you're applying to the right part of the organization.

Business or Corporate Banking

Many of the players in this group are the same ones in the consumer-banking business; others you'll find on Wall Street, not Main Street. At the highest level, the larger players (Bankers Trust, Bank of New York, and J.P. Morgan Chase & Co. are three names to add to the list of mega-players above) provide a wide range of advisory and transaction-management services to corporate clients. Depending on which institution and activity area you join, the work can resemble branch banking or investment banking.

Securities and Investments

Traditionally, this field has been the domain of a few Wall Street firms. However, as federal regulations have eased, many of the biggest commercial banks, including Bank of America, Citibank, J.P. Morgan Chase & Co., and others, have aggressively added investment-banking and asset management activities to their portfolios. For people interested in corporate finance, securities underwriting, and asset management, many of these firms offer an attractive option. However, the hiring for these positions is frequently done separately from that for corporate and consumer banking.

Nontraditional Options

Increasingly, a number of nonbank entities are offering opportunities to people interested in financial services. Players include credit card companies such as American Express, MasterCard, and Visa; credit card issuers such as Capital One and First USA; and credit-reporting agencies such as TRW. Although people at these firms are still in the money business, the specific jobs vary greatly, perhaps more widely than jobs at the traditional banks do. In particular, given the volume of transactions that many of these organizations handle, there are excellent opportunities for people with strong technical skills.

Key Jobs for MBAs

The jobs available at different commercial banks vary significantly according to the scope of their operations. Mega-banks offer a huge variety of positions, from hard-core programming spots to investment banking and trading. Small and regional banks tend to have a narrower range of more traditional positions (loan officer, teller, credit analyst, etc.).

Sales

Here's another relatively sure prospect for the uncertain future. Banks are competing with brokerages, investment banks, and mutual funds, all of which offer more obvious and alluring opportunities in sales. If you seem to have a talent for this and you'd like a chance to be a big fish earlier than all the B-school hotshots, then a bank might be just the pond for you. There is also a rising demand for salespeople who understand product development. An undergraduate degree in finance, business, or economics gets you in the door. An MBA gets you a second interview.

Salary range: $30,000 to $100,000 or more (commissions and new business you bring in can add substantially to these figures).

Trust Officer

Give this area a shot if you have a flair for financial counseling and if you like hobnobbing with high-net-worth individuals (folks with serious money). The job involves helping clients with trust services, estate planning, taxes, investing, and probate law. Warning: Sooner or later you'll find yourself in the middle of family squabbles, jealousies, disinheritances, and lawsuits. This job requires diplomacy, tact, deference, and a better, more current understanding of tax law than most attorneys need.

Salary range: $35,000 to $100,000.

Job Prospects

Two of the major trends in banking in the past decade or more have been consolidation (e.g., the acquisition of Bank One by J.P. Morgan Chase, or the takeover of FleetBoston by Bank of America) and the increasing use of technology (e.g., online banking, or automated check processing). Both of these trends have had and will continue to have a negative effect on job growth in the industry.

But it's not all bad news in banking; the U.S. population is growing, and new population centers are emerging all the time, so there will be new jobs available in new locations. And while opportunities for bank tellers and back-office clerical workers stagnate, financial analysts, financial advisors, and trust officers will enjoy growing opportunities as the (now-rich) Baby Boom generation ages.

With the Glass-Steagall Act overturned, and the convergence of the securities, banking, and insurance industries, banks now sell all kinds of financial products and services that they couldn't in the past—and face new competition for traditional lending business. This means more opportunity for financial services sales reps and less opportunity for loan officers and others with only a limited knowledge of the full array of financial products banks can now sell.

Finally, expect strong growth for tech positions in banking, as processes and operations become increasingly automated and companies' networks grow and grow.

Key Commercial Banks by 2003 Revenue

Company	Revenue ($M)	1-Yr. Change (%)	Employees
Citigroup	94,713	2	259,000
Credit Suisse Group*	65,804	−2	78,457
HSBC Holdings	56,077	39	232,000
Deutsche Bank	54,064	−7	67,682
BNP Paribas	52,096	8	89,100
UBS	49,961	8	69,000
Bank of America	49,006	6	133,549
J.P. Morgan Chase	44,363	2	110,453
Wells Fargo	31,800	12	140,000
Mizuho Financial Group	28,719	−28	27,900
Wachovia	24,474	4	86,670
Bank One	20,724	−7	71,196
U.S. Bancorp	14,571	−6	51,377
Bank of Nova Scotia	13,089	11	43,986
TD Bank	11,849	11	41,934
MBNA	11,684	12	28,000
Bank of Montreal	9,969	19	33,993
National City Corp.	9,594	10	33,331
SunTrust Banks	7,072	−6	27,578
BB&T Corp.	6,244	2	26,300

*2002 figures.

Sources: Financial Services Fact Book; Hoover's; WetFeet analysis.

Additional Resources

American Banker Online (www.americanbanker.com/index.html)

American Bankers Association (www.aba.com)

Knowledge @ Wharton: Finance and Investment
(knowledge.wharton.upenn.edu/category.cfm?catid=1)

McKinsey Quarterly: Financial Services
(www.mckinseyquarterly.com/category_editor.asp?L2=10)

Ohio State University List of Finance Sites
(www.cob.ohio-state.edu/fin/journal/jofsites.htm)

Computer Hardware

Industry Overview

Raise your hand if you still use a typewriter. Didn't think so. Despite the occasional slump in computer sales, computers are here to stay.

Computer hardware, as we use the term, means central processing units (CPUs), including memory and storage—in other words, the machine on which you run an operating system and application software and to which you attach peripherals, such as printers and fax machines.

Computer hardware and software are useless without each other. But working together they store, modify, and exchange data: words, pictures, and numbers—everything from correspondence to news photos, from drawings of jet aircraft to shipping manifests, from news releases to financial reports, from census statistics to stock quotes, from maps to movies.

The competition among computer hardware companies is particularly intense. On the one hand, in the traditional-PC market, companies' products have largely become commodified, resulting in constant downward price pressure (and narrowing profit margins). On the other hand, markets for innovative new products, such as tablet PCs, are not yet commodified. Here, the race is to develop products at breakneck speed so you can be first to market. And if a company falters, it instantly becomes a target for larger companies looking to acquire new businesses. No doubt about it: Computer hardware is a cutthroat business.

There are definite geographic concentrations in the hardware industry despite its worldwide reach. It's often noted that high-tech companies are usually located near colleges and universities, and there's a good deal of truth to that, as many companies come out of research done at such institutions. Silicon Valley is near San Jose State, the University of California at Berkeley, and Stanford University. Route 128 is near the educational mecca of Cambridge, Massachusetts. Research Triangle in North Carolina and the area around Austin, Texas, are also good examples. Still, there are other places within North America where you'll find major companies; for example, Gateway is in North Dakota.

Most major corporations in computer hardware reach across national borders. International sales normally account for a large percentage of most hardware companies' bottom lines, and India, Japan, China, and Ireland are hotbeds of hardware manufacturing.

After the tech bust of the early 2000s, the demand for computers of all flavors, from servers to PCs, evaporated as companies around the world found themselves with too much computer hardware on their hands and cash-strapped consumers became reluctant to buy or upgrade PCs. But things now seem to be turning around. Worldwide PC shipments are expected to increase by 13.5 percent in 2004. The job market in tech probably won't ever again be as good as it was in the 1990s, but at least you can finally find open tech jobs again.

Trends

Outsourcing

In the hardware world, an increasing number of manufacturers are outsourcing product and component development and manufacturing overseas. Some companies are only doing top-level design in the United States, leaving production and more basic design tasks to cheaper labor in the Philippines, China, and elsewhere. What this means is that product managers and project heads may have to travel a lot more than in previous generations; it also means that many North America–based jobs are being lost.

Consolidation

The boom of the '90s, with stock prices soaring, gave many large corporations the capital to purchase wholesale smaller (or sometimes larger) companies—even, sometimes, competing companies. For example, Compaq bought Digital Equipment Corp., and shortly after, HP bought Compaq. During the digestion process, key technologies get killed off, divisions get axed, and often so-called synergies don't work out. The result is fewer employment opportunities (unless you're a merger manager).

The Death of the PC?

Some experts predict that, in coming years, the PC will become less and less relevant. Instead, people will own smaller, cheaper, more task-specific pieces of hardware that, rather than containing tons of computing power, will work by being hooked into the Web or private networks, where all the computing power will reside. The mantra, these folks insist, will shift from "a computer on every desk" to "a network hook-up in every room."

Already, we're seeing signs that this may indeed be the future of computer hardware. Some software applications are available online on a rental basis. Online gaming is growing like gangbusters. And products like PDAs and cell phones are looking more and more like specialized mini-PCs, with wireless Internet access and networking capabilities. What this means is that, to survive, computer hardware companies may eventually have to shift their focus from making and selling PCs to making and selling innovative products that we can't even envision yet.

How It Breaks Down

For job seekers, one way to segment the industry is by the type of computer hardware the company makes. Other differentiating factors include industry and application focus and sales-and-distribution methodology: mail order, Internet, or retail.

Workstations (Desktop and Laptop)

This is perhaps the most publicly visible segment of the high-tech hardware market, with computers becoming more and more common at work, home, labs, and school. Established players here include Dell, Gateway, and Apple, which make desktop and portable computers, and companies such as Sun and SGI, which make powerful specialized workstations used in 3D rendering, molecular modeling, computer-aided design (CAD), and video editing. Portable computers represent a growing overall share of the personal computer market.

Peripherals

A peripheral is usually understood to be an external product added to a computer, such as a new mouse, speakers, CD-RW burners, and the like (check Kensington, Logitech, KeyTronic, etc.), all the way up to monitors, scanners, and printers. However, a peripheral can also be something added into a computer, such as a 3D video card or an internal modem.

Servers

There are many types of servers—those big boxes that, among other things, are the glue that holds the Internet together. In addition to Web servers, which pass back and forth all of the HTML and image files that end up on your screen, there are local area network (LAN) servers, wide area network (WAN) servers, file servers, mail servers, database servers, and more. Every time two computers (in this context, termed "clients") connect over a network, a server is involved.

As a result, servers play a critical role in business, entertainment, and education—and entire industries have sprung up to ensure that individual server products, both hardware and software, are bulletproof. Companies such as IBM, Dell, HP, and others offer "big iron" hardware and often accompany product sales with service contracts of engineering teams to install and maintain the servers. Some companies such as Oracle sell specialized hardware/software installations for databases; SAP does similar setups for companies needing to manage production and inventory.

Key Jobs for MBAs

Product Manager

As a product manager, you're a key player in coming up with product ideas and working with engineers to make them a reality. This position requires some grasp of technical matters, the ability to build consensus and teamwork, and a knack for spotting—and anticipating—market trends. Most of these jobs require an MBA or comparable experience.

Salary range: $75,000 to $150,000.

Financial Analyst

Financial analysis in computer hardware companies can take many forms: numerical analysis for production planning, industrial operations management, or general finance and accounting. In some cases, an analyst evaluates other companies as potential merger or acquisition targets. Depending on how the analyst position is defined, an MBA may be necessary.

Salary range: $35,000 to $80,000.

Job Prospects

In the last few years, the job market has been tight to an almost unprecedented degree. However, people moving from job to job is still a fairly common occurrence, and this results in regular turnover and openings. As always, keep your eyes open.

Opportunities in the computer hardware industry are not only for engineers and others with technical skills, but also for people with financial, marketing, sales, and product management backgrounds. Job seekers with technical expertise and a computer science degree attract the most opportunities and the sweetest compensation packages, whether they work as engineers, product managers, or in marketing. Opportunities in fields such as sales, customer support, and technical writing go to individuals with good people skills, a strong customer-service bias, and the ability to communicate complex ideas in plain English. If that sounds like you, give computer hardware a close look—but be prepared to get up to speed on the technical side of the hardware.

High-tech companies are generally more active and open with regard to their job openings. Their own websites are valuable resources as to vacancies, and the corporations usually maintain a high recruiting presence at colleges and universities. Don't overlook internships—in addition to providing training, companies often hire from within their intern pool. Even if you're not interested in working for the Megacorp that is offering a summer program, what you learn there adds to your value in the eyes of smaller companies.

Additional Resources

Association for Computing Machinery (www.acm.org)

Computer and Communications Industry Association (www.ccianet.org)

ComputerWorld (www.computerworld.com)

Information Technology Association of America (www.itaa.org)

Virtual Institute of Information (www.vii.org)

Key U.S. Computer Hardware Manufacturers by 2003 Revenue

Company	Revenue ($M)	1-Yr. Change (%)	Employees
IBM	89,131	10	255,157
HP	73,061	29	142,000
Hitachi, Ltd.	69,343	15	320,528
Sony Corporation	63,264	11	161,100
Samsung Electronics	49,651	103	50,000
Dell Computer Corp.	41,444	17	46,000
Fujitsu Limited	38,529	2	157,044
Cisco Systems	18,878	0	34,000
Xerox	14,704	−7	61,100
Sun Microsystems	11,434	−9	36,100
Seagate Technology	6,486	7	43,000
EMC Corp.	6,237	15	20,000
Apple Computer	6,207	8	10,912
NCR	5,598	0	29,000
Acer Inc.	4,623	51	39,000
Pitney Bowes	4,577	4	32,474
Gateway	3,402	−18	7,407
Symbol Technologies	1,530	9	5,300
Cadence Design Systems	1,120	−13	4,800
MPC Computers	1,000	n/a	1,000

Sources: Hoover's; WetFeet analysis.

Computer Software

Industry Overview

Computer software products accomplish discrete tasks and are sold as complete packages. Computer software is distinct from enterprise software, which is usually sold as part of a large (and expensive) system integration/consulting project to automate entire business processes. Some computer software products are applications, such as word processing and Web browsing. Computer software also includes operating systems, such as Windows, and utilities.

Businesses and individual consumers are the main purchasers of computer software, which is sold through both retail and business-to-business channels. In either case, companies that sell computer software are intensely focused on the needs and desires of customers. The quickest way to talk yourself out of a job in this segment is to make the technology seem more important than the end user.

Marketing is critical to the success of any computer software product, partly because there are so many companies competing in the software market and partly because computers are still new to a lot of people. In fact, in most companies that produce computer software, the marketing department calls the shots.

At the other end of the totem pole, technical writers are employed at most computer software companies to write user documentation, either for publication in the form of manuals or, increasingly, as online help. The industry also employs— in descending order of technical expertise—software testers, customer service reps, sales personnel, and staff for the usual coterie of business functions, from HR to accounting.

Trends

Linux

Linux system software, the centerpiece of the open-source movement (which champions free software for all and welcomes and encourages developer contributions to the free software), is finally making a splash in the business world. More companies, such as Credit Suisse First Boston and Merrill Lynch, are seeing the benefits of not having to pay for software and upgrades and beginning to adopt Linux environments. Computer makers such as Dell and Hewlett-Packard are shipping PCs and servers loaded with Linux. And big business-software providers such as BEA Systems, SAP, and Veritas are making products that run on Linux.

The Internet

The Internet has meant a sea change in the software industry. Many software users now download their purchases from software providers' websites, forgoing diskettes and packaging and getting straight to business. And the subscription ASP (application service provider) model (a.k.a. the pay-as-you-go model), in which users access software and databases that are stored on the vendors' servers via the Web, is proving attractive in areas from gaming to business software. Indeed, companies including Oracle, Siebel Systems, and Salesforce.com are all seeing success using the pay-as-you-go model.

Consolidation

The software industry has been teeming with M&A activity of late. Business Objects recently purchased Crystal Decisions, Hyperion Solutions bought Brio, EMC bought Documentum and VMware, and Oracle is trying to acquire PeopleSoft. The reason for all this activity: Buying competitors is a good way to increase market share—and buying them now, at the beginning of an expected economic recovery, is smarter than buying them after their stock prices have risen too far.

How It Breaks Down

The computer software market is most commonly segmented according to the type of work a product does. A few of the major market segments are listed below, along with the names of a few companies that are active in each.

System Software

Microsoft's Windows is by far the dominant example in his category—but not the only one. Apple's MacOS is still alive and well, and Unix, including Linux, is a force in the server market. HP, Sun Microsystems, IBM, and Silicon Graphics provide versions of Unix with servers they manufacture. Red Hat has actually made a business out of selling a version of Linux, which is also available free on the Internet.

Productivity

Personal productivity includes word processing, spreadsheets, presentations, database management, graphic design, and other applications that help people do their jobs. Key players: Adobe (PageMaker, PhotoShop, Illustrator), Microsoft (Word, PowerPoint, Excel).

Education

Educational software helps your kids learn to read, teaches you about geography or a foreign language, stimulates logical thinking, and so on. This category also comprises children's educational games, the nascent electronic-book industry, teaching resources, and music instruction. Key players: The Learning Company, Cendant Corporation, Disney.

Finance

Financial software includes applications for small business and personal accounting, personal finance, and tax preparation. Key players: Intuit (maker of Quicken), Block Financial (the Kiplinger titles), Microsoft.

Internet

Internet software includes more than the two leading browsers, which are produced by Netscape and Microsoft. Sun Microsystems and some other companies dream of breaking Microsoft's dominance by developing software that you don't buy. Instead, you rent it as needed, downloading it via the Internet. This category also includes software for creating websites, from companies such as Macromedia.

Utilities

Utilities help you keep your computer running by diagnosing and fixing problems. Symantec (Norton Utilities) is a leading developer.

Games

A highly competitive and extremely broad market segment, this includes role-playing software, auto and flight simulation, sports, strategy games such as chess, and children's games. Key players: Electronic Arts, GT Interactive, Hasbro Interactive, Broderbund. Also, note that there are many small, thriving studios that use the bigger players for distribution and marketing, as well as big-name individual designers—Sid Meyer, Ron Martinez, Will Wright, Jim Gasperini—who will work for game companies on a project-by-project basis.

Reference

Homes, schools, and businesses are getting rid of old bound reference collections in favor of CD-ROM reference tools that offer portability, lightning-fast searches, and interactive media. This market segment includes encyclopedias, dictionaries, atlases, Internet guides, and zip code directories. Key players: Microsoft, Grolier Interactive.

Key Job for MBAs

Product or Project Manager

Product managers take the software title from conception through development to the finished product. You define the features that the product will encompass and work with teams of designers, engineers, writers, and quality assurance testers. Product managers typically hold MBAs or have extensive experience in the software field.

Salary range: $55,000 to $90,000, with more-senior product managers (with 3 to 5 years' experience) making $70,000 to $110,000.

Job Prospects

The disappearance of many start-ups and Web-based companies, plus tech-industry consolidation, has resulted in layoffs and lower unemployment levels than this industry enjoyed in the 1990s. But computer technology changes rapidly, and the industry is sure to rebound as the economy recovers. The Bureau of Labor Statistics predicts that occupations in the computer software industry will be one of the fastest growing between 2003 and 2010.

Much of the activity in computer software is happening in Silicon Valley, but you also might check out opportunities in other high-tech regions including Boston, Austin, Minneapolis, New York City, Denver, Dallas, Atlanta, Boca Raton, and the Research Triangle region of North Carolina.

If you're looking for international work experience, give consumer software a close look. Foreign markets are the next big thing for software companies, who are now focusing their sights on China, Japan, Southeast Asia, Germany, and the United Kingdom. Note, however, that these opportunities are usually limited to sales and marketing, and even in these areas, culture and language differences are such that local talent usually takes precedence.

Key Computer Software Companies by 2003 Revenue

Company	Revenue ($M)	1-Yr. Change (%)	Employees
IBM	89,131	10	255,157
Hewlett-Packard	73,061	29	142,000
Microsoft	32,187	14	55,000
Sun Microsystems	11,434	–9	36,100
Oracle	9,475	–2	40,650
SAP	8,831	13	30,251
Lucent	8,470	–31	34,500
Nintendo	4,203	1	2,977
Computer Associates	3,116	5	16,000
Sungard Data Systems	2,955	14	10,000
Electronic Arts	2,482	44	4,000
PeopleSoft	2,267	16	12,163
Veritas Software	1,771	18	5,647
Symantec	1,407	31	4,300
Compuware	1,375	–20	9,356
Siebel Systems	1,354	–17	4,972
SAS Institute	1,340	14	9,251
BMC Software	1,327	3	6,861
Adobe	1,295	11	3,507
Cadence Design Systems	1,120	–13	4,800

Sources: Hoover's; WetFeet analysis.

Additional Resources

ComputerWorld (www.computerworld.com)

Developer.com (www.developer.com)

Internet.com (www.internet.com)

Software and Information Industry Association (www.siia.net)

Consulting

Industries

Industry Overview

So, you're about to graduate, and you think you want to be a management consultant. Or, more likely, you think you'll spend a few years as a consultant and then move on to other things. You're not alone. Consulting firms are traditionally among the largest employers of top MBA and college graduates. But with single-digit growth projected for the industry in 2004 and 2005, expect competition for jobs to remain tough.

More than half the people in top MBA programs and a significant number of college seniors flirt with the idea of becoming a management consultant after graduation. It's a high-paying, high-profile field that offers students the opportunity to take on a lot of responsibility right out of school and quickly learn a great deal about the business world.

In essence, consultants are hired advisors to corporations. They tackle a wide variety of business problems and provide solutions for their clients. Depending on the size and chosen strategy of the firm, these problems can be as straightforward as researching a new market or as complex as totally rethinking the client's organization. No matter what the engagement is, the power that management consultants wield is hard to scoff at. They can advise a client to acquire a related company worth hundreds of millions of dollars, or reduce the size of its workforce by thousands of employees.

Management consultants must be skilled at conducting research and analyzing it. Research means collecting raw data from a variety of sources including the client's computers, trade associations in the client's industry, government agencies, and, perhaps most importantly, surveys and market studies that you devise and implement yourself. It also means interviewing people to gather anecdotal information and expert opinion. The interviewees may be anyone, from industry experts to the client's top executives to the client's lowest-level employees. All this data must then be analyzed, using tools from spreadsheets to your own brain. The idea here is to spot behavior patterns, production bottlenecks, market movements, and other trends and conditions that affect a client's business.

Your ultimate job is to improve the client's business by effecting changes in response to your analysis. That's the hard part, because it involves convincing the client to accept your recommendations, often in the face of opposition from client executives who resent outsiders upstaging them with the boss or resistance from company employees who have something to lose from change. To succeed you'll need excellent people skills and the ability to put together a persuasive PowerPoint presentation. Finally, you'll need the ability to handle disappointment if your solution fails or the client decides not to even try implementing it.

One good thing about the advice business: Companies always seem to want more. As evidence, the consulting industry has been on a sustained growth binge for well more than a decade. One other thing about the consulting business: The product really is the people, and firms compete on the basis of who's the smartest and the hardest working. As a result, each firm wants to hire the best and the brightest. If you're one of them—you probably know if you are—you'll have a good shot at landing one of these competitive jobs.

Trends

Each consulting firm has a set of new programs and developments. However, you should familiarize yourself with a number of industry-wide trends. If you're interested in a particular firm, explore the role the following industry trends are playing in its practice.

The Rise of RFID

Wal-Mart and Tesco, the largest retailers in the United States, and the Department of Defense (DoD), one of the world's largest buyers of IT services, plan to require that suppliers add radio frequency identification (RFID) tags to pallets, cases, and cartons of material—creating a potential bonanza for consultants. RFID lets retailers track buying trends—information that helps them put in accurate orders and change marketing to meet demand. RFID is becoming progressively less expensive, and is easier than bar codes, because the RFID tags don't require line of site to be read. Manufacturers are hiring consultants to understand what they must do to meet the requirements and how the new technology can help their companies operate more efficiently. While many are in reactionary mode, no doubt consulting firms will soon be working with them to implement RFID to save money and generate greater profits. AMR Research estimates RFID will generate about $1.2 billion in business in 2006, up from about $400 million in 2003. RFID also has potential Big Brother–type applications— the DoD could use a car's spark plug, for instance, to track where somebody drives. IBM and Accenture are current leaders in this field.

Public to Private

Last year, *Consultants News* reported that between 2002 and 2005, the government sector was poised for double-digit growth, much of it thanks to the Office of Homeland Security. After 9/11, a number of firms, including American Management Systems, BearingPoint, Booz Allen, EDS, and IBM Global Services, rushed to offer homeland security consulting. In 2004, however, public sector business appears to be slowing down, with analysts suggesting financial services will make a comeback. This could hurt the bottom line of some of the public sector winners, such as BearingPoint and Booz Allen, but it will undoubtedly help that of many others.

Tsk, Tsk, Tsk

In recent years, consulting firms have been finding themselves in hot water for ethical transgressions—and this past year was no exception. Among some of this year's highlights:

- IBM was accused of bribing South Korean government officials, who helped it win tens of millions of dollars in government contracts.

- Capgemini faces a lawsuit for overbilling millions of dollars. The case alleges the firm billed clients for the full retail price of travel expenses though it had negotiated discounts of up to 50 percent and that these transgressions took place over a 10-year period. PricewaterhouseCoopers, now a part of IBM Global Services, was also named in the suit, and settled its part for a sweet $54 million. KPMG and BearingPoint, also named, settled for $17 million each.

- BearingPoint was accused of having an unfair competitive advantage by a federal investigation. After helping to write specifications for developing a "competitive private sector" in Iraq, BearingPoint got the $240 million contract, which seemed to suggest a conflict of interest.

- Deloitte's Italian practice allegedly ignored and hid accounting anomalies at Parmalat, but the company denies wrongdoing.

Return of the Accountants?

The first phase of Ernst & Young's noncompete agreement with Capgemini ran out in 2003, and the audit firm is rebuilding its consulting capabilities with an emphasis on health-care consulting. If it succeeds, KPMG (whose noncompete with BearingPoint runs until February 2006) and PricewaterhouseCoopers (whose agreement with IBM extends until the second half of 2007) might follow suit. Stay tuned.

The Challenge to Outsourcing

Outsourcing has been one of the greatest revenue builders for many of the IT firms such as Accenture, but a number of India-based firms, such as Infosys, are getting in on the game. These players can charge $30 an hour versus the $150 IBM Global Services, Accenture, and EDS must charge. To counter their overseas rivals, some consulting firms are throwing in hardware and other consulting services to sweeten their bids. It doesn't seem to be enough to bridge the gap: Indian firms have advantages on both cost and quality. Look for North American firms to begin acquiring Indian firms (which is what IBM did with Daksh eServices, one of the world's largest call center operations) as well as Indian outsourcing to boom.

How It Breaks Down

People who want a career in consulting can find a number of attractive choices. To help you get a better handle on the options, we've grouped the consulting world into several different segments. Keep in mind, however, that our groupings are flexible. Firms in one group can and do compete directly with players in other segments. Also, consolidation, growth, and market gyrations rapidly change the landscape. One final caveat: Where we've placed a firm does not reflect the quality of the organization. Brief profiles of a few of the major categories follow.

Elite Management Consulting Firms

This group is populated by a few top strategy firms—Bain, Booz Allen, BCG, McKinsey—and a host of smaller challengers. The bulk of the work done by these firms consists of providing strategic or operational advice to top executive officers in Fortune 500 companies. For this, they charge the highest fees and enjoy the most prestige. They also have the biggest attitudes, work the most intense hours, and take home the most pay. The elite management consulting firms fight to woo the top graduates from the best graduate and undergraduate schools. Although some elite firms differentiate themselves by specializing in particular industries or functions, most consultants who work for this group of firms are generalists who work on a wide variety of projects and industries.

Big Four–Affiliated Consulting Firms

The Big Four were the Big Five until Andersen went bankrupt after the Enron scandal, driving what at the time seemed to be the final stake into the heart of a historically lucrative marriage between consultants and auditors. When Andersen went bankrupt, consulting firms were already separating from their audit partners: Ernst & Young had sold its consulting practice to Cap Gemini to form Cap Gemini Ernst & Young (now Capgemini) and KPMG Consulting had broken off from its accounting side and gone public (it has since changed its name to BearingPoint). Other members of this group include PricewaterhouseCoopers, which sold its consulting unit to IBM in July 2002, and Deloitte Consulting, where a buyout by consulting partners was scotched (the consulting arm has since been reintegrated into Deloitte). This past year, there were whispers about accounting firms rebuilding their consulting practices, as some of the conflict-of-interest issues have faded. The Big Four firms offer strategic advice, information systems support, and other more specialized consulting services to many of the same corporations served by the elite consulting firms. They also boast strong information technology capabilities on projects requiring heavy systems implementation work, and in some cases offer outsourcing to compete with the technology and systems consulting firms.

Boutique Strategy Firms

Within the universe of strategy and operations, consulting firms constitute a significant subgroup of firms that specialize in a particular industry, process, or type of consulting. Although it encompasses too many firms to name, this group includes players that have expertise in particular fields. If you're interested in a particular industry or type of consulting, these firms offer excellent career opportunities. Typically, they're smaller than the big-name strategy firms and work with a more specialized group of clients—so they won't usually require you to work in industries that don't interest you. Insiders tell us that working for one of these firms may give you more marketable experience if you decide to leave the world of consulting.

Examples of boutique firms are Cornerstone Research (litigation support), Gartner Group (high-tech research), and Pittiglio Rabin Todd & McGrath (high-tech operations).

Technology and Systems Consulting Firms

If you're technologically inclined and love designing computer systems and applications, this might be the area for you. Firms here typically take on large projects to design, implement, and manage their clients' information and computer systems. In contrast to pie-in-the-sky strategy consulting, which involves work that can often be done at the home office, technology consulting often takes place in the bowels of the client organization. A typical project might involve creating a new inventory tracking system for a national retailer. Such a project might include analyzing the client's informational needs, acquiring new hardware, writing computer code to run the new system, and syncing the systems to deliver information in real time over the Internet. In general, this kind of consulting job requires large teams of people who actually do the computer work. As a result, there are usually more opportunities for people from undergraduate or technical backgrounds than from MBA backgrounds, and it's not the same high-prestige work strategy consultants are known for. Technology and systems firms have also moved aggressively to take on business-process outsourcing in order to manage elements of a client's business, such as a call center. In most cases, these jobs pay less than those at the top strategy firms.

Human Resources Consulting

Technology's not your thing? How about the other end of the spectrum? A number of consulting firms specialize in providing human resources advice. This can include everything from designing an employee evaluation and compensation system to conducting organizational effectiveness training to helping an organization through a significant change event, such as a merger. Because such work is so important, HR consulting firms often work with relatively senior employees at client organizations. HR consultants often work as long and travel as much as their counterparts in general management consulting.

Representative firms include Accenture (Change Management Group), Buck Consultants, Deloitte, Hay Group, Hewitt Associates, Mercer Human Resource Consulting, Towers Perrin, and Wyatt Group.

Key Jobs for MBAs

As each firm has its favorite buzzwords, it also has unique terminology for its rank and file. While the titles might vary from firm to firm, the roles can basically be divided up as follows: analyst (also called research associate or staff consultant at some firms), consultant (or senior consultant), manager, and partner or VP.

Associate/Consultant/Senior Consultant

This is the typical port of entry for newly minted MBAs (and increasingly for non-MBA graduate students as well). Senior consultants often perform research and analysis, formulate recommendations, and present findings to the client. Oh, and at many firms, they have to implement those great ideas, too. Although this is usually a tenure-track position, a fair number of consultants will leave the business after 2 or 3 years to pursue entrepreneurial or industry positions.

Salary range: $65,000 to $130,000 or more with bonus.

Manager

After a few years, a senior consultant will move up to manager. As the title implies, this usually means leading a team of consultants and analysts toward project completion. Some firms may hire MBAs with significant work experience directly into the manager position, particularly in their IT practices. In addition to having more rigorous responsibilities for managing the project team, the manager will typically be a primary point person for client interactions.

Salary range: $70,000 to $150,000.

Partner or VP

Congratulations! You've forded the River Jordan of consulting and arrived at the Promised Land. Note that some firms further subdivide partners into junior and senior grade. And, if you aspire to it, there's always that chairman or CEO position. As a partner, one of your big responsibilities will be to sell new work. Fortunately, as with other big-ticket sales jobs, the pay can be quite rewarding.

Salary range: $250,000 to several million dollars at leading firms.

Job Outlook

After several down years, firms began recruiting again in 2004. The economic recovery kicked in around August to September 2003, and is expected to drive single-digit growth for the consulting industry through 2006. "I think [2004] is a year of renewed growth for the consulting industry, which means a period of renewed growth for recruiting as well," one insider says. Firms are reporting more contract wins and utilization rates well above the norm. "The outlook is positive," another insider says. "We see a movement upward in hiring numbers. We're seeing a lot more deals, and our capacity is at the highest mark that it's been in a couple of years. The management team absolutely thinks the work will continue."

The growth that appears to have begun won't mirror that of the go-go 1990s. "I don't think we'll see the spiking growth that we saw in the late '90s," says an insider. "We moved through the early 2000s on cost reduction. Now the focus is on growth of the bottom line. The focus isn't so much on how fast I can grow my top line or how I can cut my costs, but how can I improve my productivity. I think those initiatives are going to drive the opportunities for growth in the consulting industry."

A few things are different from hiring a few years back. One, buying patterns are changing. "What I've been seeing is that the buyers are looking for less hype and more substance. Over the boom years, there were a lot of high-flying firms with a lot of hype around them," an insider says. "Now what we're seeing is a buying community that's a little more savvy, a little more senior. There's a trend that the decision to hire consultants is being moved up higher in the organization."

As a consequence, firms are looking for more experience in those they hire. "For the pre-MBA experience, it would be advantageous to make sure they're getting some serious, substantial experience—industry experience for the type of client engagements they want to work in post-MBA," an insider says. "Some MBAs will look at the summer associate program as an opportunity to try something completely different. But if they're trying something for variety, and they want to work in a post-MBA position in a field different than their summer position, they're putting themselves at a disadvantage."

Key Consulting Companies by 2003 Revenue

Company	Revenue ($M)	1-Yr. Change (%)	Employees
IBM Global Svcs	42,635	17	180,000
Electronic Data Systems Corp.	21,476	0	132,000
Computer Sciences Corp.*	14,768	30	90,000
Accenture	13,397	2	83,000
Capgemini	7,222	–2	49,805
McKinsey & Co.	3,000	–12	12,000
Deloitte Consulting	3,245	3	12,000
Mercer	2,719	15	15,900
Booz Allen Hamilton*	2,700	23	14,800
Hewitt Associates	2,031	16	15,000
BearingPoint	1,554	n/a	15,000
Boston Consulting Group	1,120	10	4,250
Towers Perrin	1,031	2	9,000
Aon Consulting	898	13	n/a
Bain & Co.	891	17	2,450
A.T. Kearney	846	–16	4,000
Watson Wyatt & Co.	710	0	4,100
Roland Berger	665	4	1,630
Navigant Consulting	318	23	1,367
Corporate Executive Board	210	30	1,222

*2004 figures.

Sources: Hoover's; *Consultants News*; WetFeet analysis.

Rank	Firm
| **Consulting Magazine's Top Five Firms to Work For, 2003**	
1	Bain & Company
2	McKinsey & Company
3	Pittiglio Rabin Todd & McGrath
4	Hewitt Associates
5	The Boston Consulting Group
Source: *Consulting Magazine*, www.consultingmag.com/CMBestFirms.html.	

Additional Resources

ConsultingCentral.com (www.consultingcentral.com)

Fuqua School of Business Consulting Club (www.duke.edu/web/fuquacc)

Institute of Management Consultants (www.imcusa.org)

Kennedy Information (www.kennedyinfo.com)

McKinsey Quarterly (www.mckinseyquarterly.com)

Consumer Electronics

Industry Overview

Think about all the consumer electronics products out there: the color TVs (not to mention the flat-screen plasma TVs), the MP3 and DVD players, the digital camcorders. Now think about all of the engineers, designers, marketers, salespeople, customer service reps, and finance gurus it takes to design, manufacture, and market all those electronic gadgets. The consumer electronics industry is big time.

Although much of the actual manufacturing is done in Asia and other low labor-cost locations, other functions have remained in the United States. On the technical side, opportunities exist for software and electronics engineers, as well as quality assurance engineers, industrial designers, manufacturing design engineers, and IT professionals. If you're a people person—if you can design a marketing campaign, close a distribution deal with a major retail chain, write marketing copy, or help a confused consumer understand a complex product—consumer electronics companies may be good places for you, too.

You can earn your stripes at a multinational corporation such as Samsung or Mitsubishi, where big money is backing big products like high-definition television (HDTV) and smart phones (a combined wireless phone/PDA). Or you can try your hand at a young start-up that's pushing the consumer electronics envelope in one market niche or another. So before you start your job search, think about whether you like the structure and resources (and bureaucracy) that a big organization will have or whether you prefer the flexibility and cutting-edge spirit (and bare-bones budget) of a new company.

Job seekers should also keep in mind that consumer electronics are global brands, so many companies have opportunities for international positions and travel, and foreign language skills are often highly desirable. And in the United States, though there is some concentration of consumer electronics jobs on the East and West Coasts, the industry is sprawled across the country. Many of the large companies have multiple offices to choose from, with each location housing a different product line or corporate function.

Trends

More than Just Entertainment

As it has gone digital, the consumer electronics industry has evolved way beyond televisions and stereos. Digitization has made possible some brand-new electronic toys, such as consumer-priced global positioning systems. And already established consumer electronics products such as PDAs (personal digital assistants; think Palm or Handspring), are coming out with expanded features such as the ability to send and receive email; digital camera capability; gaming capability; wireless network readiness; GPS capability; and cell phone capability. Consumer electronics products are insinuating themselves into the furthest recesses of our lives.

Intellectual Property Confusion

Since the first big digital consumer product, the audio CD, hit the market in the early 1980s, nothing has slowed the digital juggernaut, with one exception: worries about pirating—of music and, more recently, of movies. Such concerns delayed the introduction of writeable CD equipment (and digital audio tape), and the spread of the MP3 format for recording music and exchanging it via the Internet is giving the music industry conniptions. When Napster came on the scene, media consumers had the advantage over the entertainment industry, which feared for its massive profit-making ability. Nowadays, after fighting back (by cutting deals with computer and electronics makers to get them to include copyright-protection features in their products; by attacking file-sharing software makers; by suing downloaders and the ISPs that serve them), it seems the entertainment industry has the upper hand again.

Competition from Computer Makers

The consumer electronics industry is converging quickly with the computer industry. Each year, electronics products look more and more like computers—and companies that used to do business in one market or the other are now doing business in both. Take the PDA, TiVo, the gaming console, the cell phone with Internet access—all of these are essentially computers, with computer chips inside them and computer operating systems allowing them to work. At the same time, computer companies are moving in the direction of making devices, such as PDAs and gaming consoles, that are essentially consumer electronics products. What this means for consumer electronics companies: Much more competition from computer companies in coming years.

How It Breaks Down

The consumer electronics industry includes manufacturers of all shapes and sizes. The largest are multinational conglomerates with more than 100,000 employees and interests in many different industries. The smallest often have only one office with less than 50 employees focused on one product. In the middle are manufacturers that offer a range of products within a certain category, such as speakers and audio accessories. Because companies of all sizes can make similar products, industry observers usually break down the market by product category rather than company size.

Video

These days, all eyes are on video. As the switch is made from analog to digital technology, the market is quickly expanding beyond traditional televisions,

VCRs, and camcorders to include digital televisions, digital versatile disc (DVD) players, home theater systems, home satellite systems, and set-top Internet access devices. Key players include Matsushita (Panasonic), Philips (Magnavox), Sony, Thomson (RCA), TiVo, and Microsoft (WebTV).

Audio

Vinyl may be the latest retro resurgence, but it can't stop the digital wave. Consumers can now choose from CDs, DVDs, MiniDiscs, and MP3s (a computer file format that lets you download music from the Internet) to get digital-quality sound. The proliferation of digital formats is also driving new demand for upgraded home theater systems, multimedia PCs, car stereos, and portable players. Key players include Bose, Harman International, Sony, and Toshiba.

Mobile and Wireless

Mobile electronics and wireless technology have transformed communication. Better technology and lower prices have turned high-end products like cell phones and pagers into commodities sold out of street-side kiosks. And broad market demand is fueling the race to develop the next generation of phones, pagers, and PDAs, which will use digital cellular, digital personal communication service (PCS), and wireless modems to interconnect. High-end car audio, security, navigation, and multimedia systems manufacturers are also taking advantage of the new digital technologies and making inroads in the mass market. Key players include Motorola, Nokia, and Philips.

Multimedia

Multimedia products create an interactive experience for the user by combining sound, graphics, text, and video. The personal computer is the main delivery platform for multimedia products, although the digital television will also offer a multimedia experience. Again, digital is the word to watch. For PC users, DVD-ROMs offer better speed and storage capabilities than CD-ROMs. Digital cameras save digitized images in a memory cache, rather than on film. Software plug-ins, which can be downloaded from the Internet, let users experience streaming audio and video applications on their PCs. And new video game consoles let players interact while playing games that include robust graphics and sound. Key players include Canon, Nintendo, Sony, Microsoft, and Toshiba (DVD-ROM).

Integrated Home Systems

Picture this: While sitting at your computer at work, you pull up the website for your home, check out the live video feed to make sure your new puppy isn't devouring the muffins you forgot to put back in the cupboard this morning, click a link to preheat the oven for dinner, and turn up the thermostat to warm the house. This is the smart home. Smart homes are powered by integrated home systems—electronic products that are networked together and connected to the rest of the world via the Internet or wireless technology. Players in this fledgling market include IBM, and appliance manufacturers like Sunbeam and Whirlpool are joining the fray by experimenting with products that are networkable.

Key Jobs for MBAs

Inventing, designing, building, manufacturing, distributing, and selling consumer electronics is a big business that requires lots of people with lots of different skills. On the business side, this industry employs marketers, customer service professionals, and operations specialists.

Marketer

Marketers are the people who convince consumers to buy consumer electronics products that, let's face it, in most cases they don't really need. Responsibilities can include pricing strategy, distribution, promotion, advertising, and public relations. Marketers analyze market trends, prepare sales forecasts, manage inventory levels, and coordinate trade show preparation. Entry-level positions often require a Bachelor's degree in business or marketing, while product-management positions usually require an MBA. Candidates should have strong analytical, business-planning, and presentation skills, plus good creative judgment.

Salary range: $35,000 to $200,000.

Additional Resources

Consumer Electronics Association (www.ce.org)

Electronics Industries Alliance (www.eia.org)

Electronics Technicians Association, International (www.eta-sda.com)

Key Consumer Electronics Companies by 2003 Revenue

Company	Revenue ($M)	1-Yr. Change (%)	Employees
Hitachi	69,343	15	320,528
Sony	63,264	11	161,000
Matsushita Electric Ind.	61,681	19	288,324
Samsung Electronics	54,252	9	88,447
Toshiba	47,192	16	165,776
Fujitsu	38,529	2	157,044
Royal Philips Electronics	36,505	9	164,438
Mitsubishi Electric	30,364	10	110,279
Sanyo Electric Co.	18,949	19	79,025
LG Electronics	16,888	−9	64,000
Emerson Electric	13,958	1	106,700
Whirlpool Corp.	12,176	11	68,000
Thomson	10,635	−11	65,487
Pioneer Corp.	5,936	18	34,656
Nintendo Co.	4,203	1	2,977
Daewoo Electronics*	2,290	−9	5,110
Harman Int'l Industries	2,228	22	10,776
Kenwood Corp.	1,882	−18	4,877
Bose Corp.	1,600	23	8,000

*2002 figures.
Sources: Hoover's; WetFeet analysis.

Consumer Products

Industry Overview

Consumer products is one of those elastic phrases that can include any of the jars, boxes, cans, or tubes on your kitchen and bathroom shelves—or it can expand to include pretty much everything you charged on your Visa card last year. This industry manufactures and, perhaps more importantly, markets everything from food and beverages to toiletries and small appliances. (We do not include industries sometimes put in this category but covered in other profiles: autos, apparel, entertainment products, and consumer durables, which are large appliances and other products expected to last more than 3 years).

The consumer products industry can be divided into four groups: beverages, food, toiletries and cosmetics, and small appliances. Most firms offer products that fit primarily into only one of these groups, although a firm may have a smattering of brands that cross the lines. Virtually all companies are similar in organizational structure, emphasis on brand management, and approach to business.

Consumer products are the foundation of the modern consumer economy. The industry itself not only generates an enormous portion of the gross domestic product, it also pumps huge amounts of money into other industries, notably advertising and retail. Individual consumers make up the majority of this industry's customers; sales are concentrated in the United States, Japan, and Western Europe, though other parts of the world are working hard for the privileges of wearing clothing emblazoned with company logos, eating processed food, and chopping vegetables with an electric motor instead of a traditional utensil. Success in consumer products is all about marketing an individual product, often by promoting a brand name. The competition is ferocious for shelf space, so package design, marketing, and customer satisfaction are key elements.

The majority of companies that sell consumer packaged goods are conglomerates consisting of many diverse subsidiaries selling brands that consumers recognize. Sara Lee Corporation produces products from Ball Park franks to Hanes underwear to Endust furniture polish. Unilever, an industry giant based in England, sells teas and soups, pasta and pizza sauces, ice cream, bath soaps, shampoo, salad dressing, margarine, laundry detergent, toothpaste, cosmetics, frozen foods, and perfumes. Other big players in the industry include Nestle, Clorox, Kraft, Procter & Gamble, S.C. Johnson, and ConAgra.

Trends

Size Matters

A spate of mergers and acquisitions in recent years has resulted in a smaller group of larger giants—this is not an industry with a lot of boutique enterprises and garage entrepreneurs. (Recent industry acquisitions include PepsiCo's purchase of Quaker Oats, Kraft's purchase of Nabisco, and General Mills's purchase of Pillsbury.) There's no doubt about it: The conglomerates hold the power positions in this industry. Size gives them economies of scale, and a diversity of products gives them protection against down cycles. Which is not to say that cute little mail-order pickle-and-jam companies don't crop up every now and then and make a serious go of it. They do. These places aren't where the majority of the jobs are, however—at least not until Unilever or Nestle takes them over.

Chasing the Niches

The demographics of the United States are changing. For example, the number of under-18s of Hispanic descent is now greater than the number of white under-18s—and many of them speak Spanish as a first language. Consumer products companies are desperate to reach the Hispanic and other niche markets, and that means altering traditional product-development and marketing techniques to create products that will be in demand in those markets and sell to them as effectively as possible. Sophisticated market research allows brand managers to better understand niche markets and how to market to them. And computers and the Internet make it easier for companies to market their products to different niches in different ways.

Globalization

Like many other industries, the consumer products industry is rapidly globalizing. Companies based in the United States have operations around the world that are involved in producing products for both domestic and foreign markets. For example, a company may collect the raw materials that go into its products in one country, refine those raw materials in another country, and assemble the refined materials into finished products in a third company—in effect, doing only product design and marketing in the United States.

This has been going on for a number of years now. Companies like it because it lowers their costs. Employees? Well, they don't like it when their jobs are eliminated in the United States and replaced by cheaper workers overseas. Meanwhile, the antiglobalization crowd is growing like crazy, meaning that we've probably only just begun to see protests and boycotts of companies accused of exploiting third-world people and places, as well as American workers, in their quest for lower costs.

How It Breaks Down

Beverages

Intensely competitive and hugely reliant on advertising, this is a mature industry. Different segments of the beverage world include beer (Adolph Coors, Anheuser-

Busch, Phillip Morris, Miller, Stroh's), soft drinks (Coca-Cola, PepsiCo, Cadbury Schweppes, National Beverage), and juices (Minute Maid by Coca-Cola).

Foods

There may be a little less consolidation in the food industry than in beverages, but this is also a mature and competitive industry with single-digit growth. Most of the packaged goods that fill our pantries, cupboards, and refrigerators come from a handful of big-league corporate players. Some are household names: Campbell Soup, Dole, General Mills, H.J. Heinz, and Kellogg have spent enormous sums of money to imprint their names on your brain. Other big players, such as Kraft and ConAgra (Hunt's, Healthy Choice, and Wesson) are better known for brands they own.

Toiletries, Cosmetics, and Cleaning Products

Baby boomers aren't getting any younger, and vanity will outlast us all. So will household dirt. So this is a solid category for the foreseeable future. At three-and-one-half times the size of its nearest competitor, Procter & Gamble is the Godzilla of this group—and indeed the consumer products world in general. Other players include Avon Products, Clorox, Colgate-Palmolive, Revlon, Gillette, Kimberly-Clark (Huggies, Kotex, and Kleenex), Unilever, Johnson & Johnson, and S.C. Johnson (Pledge, Glade, and Windex).

Small Appliances

This is an amalgam of companies in various industries. More people are building and buying homes, and forecasters don't expect the trend to slow. So tools, kitchen gadgets, air conditioners, chain saws, and anything else Saturday shoppers enjoy pausing over in the hardware store are selling well, and the future looks rosy for this segment of the industry. Nevertheless, this is also a relatively mature industry, and the brand system is not as strong as it is in the categories mentioned above. Players here include Black & Decker, Sunbeam, Sears, and Snap-On.

Key Jobs for MBAs

This is a hierarchical business and though merit and hard work count for a lot, even the wunderkinds have to do time before they're promoted. Senior management positions in marketing, operations, R&D, and other departments tend to be filled from within the company (or at least, from within the industry).

Marketing Assistant or Analyst

If you've just graduated from college, these are the trenches that prepare you for product management and brand management. Some of the work here is administrative, but your ideas are welcome and the brand management team will depend on your organizational ability as much as your knowledge of the target customer. An MBA will typically start as an assistant brand manager for a few years before being put in charge of shepherding all the product pieces to market. In either case, you can expect a lot of poring over sales and merchandising figures, Nielsen ratings, and premiums. Compensation varies widely depending on the company and its location, as well as where you went to school and your relevant experience.

Salary range: $25,000 to $70,000.

Product or Brand Manager

Conjure up your gloomiest images of what shopping was like in the Soviet Union. This is the fate product managers work to save us from. They create the catchy new names and novel packaging. They ask prospective customers how to make products even more irresistible. Then they scramble like mad for prominent display space, ad dollars, and their marketing director's active support. You either work your way up the ladder to these jobs or start at this rung with an MBA. Very important reminder: Headhunters really love successful product managers.

Salary range: $50,000 to $100,000.

Market Researcher

To do this job, you don't really have to wear glasses and ask silly questions—you do have to have a strong interest in the psychology of customer behavior and an ability to coax this information out of prospective purchasers. Tools of the trade include focus groups, one-on-one interviews, Nielsen data, and quantitative surveys. People can enter these positions from undergraduate, MBA, or industry backgrounds.

Salary range: $30,000 to $100,000.

Manufacturing or Finance Manager

Because of the just-in-time inventory pressures, manufacturing and production plants also increasingly need MBAs with creative financing skills to help solve problems, assess profitability, and acquire new businesses. In some companies, these finance analysts and managers actually have equal and occasionally even greater authority than marketers. They aren't responsible for the presentations to senior management or the coordination with advertising, but they make many of the important recommendations and decisions that direct the course of new product development.

Salary range: $50,000 to $90,000.

Job Prospects

Professional job opportunities in this industry are largely in brand management, sales, customer service, and market research and development. And constantly emerging new products and increasing competition promise to provide positions for brand managers and marketers from now until the end of time.

The mammoth consumer products companies often recruit on campus and boast strong training programs for recent college grads, but they're also known to pull experienced people from other firms in the consumer products industry. If you choose to remain in the industry for a long time—and many people do—you can spend time overseas, try out new products and categories, and ultimately move into general management. Although you'll probably lead a less glamorous life than any of your pals in banking or consulting, this is an industry in which you can have real profit-and-loss responsibility, earn a very comfortable salary, and get home from the office while there's still daylight, at least during summer.

On the downside, there are areas in the industry with less-certain futures. Technology is sure to eliminate large chunks of workers, as functions like production, packaging, and customer service become increasingly automated or migrate overseas to cheaper labor pools.

Additional Resources

The Beverage Network (www.bevnet.com)

Cosmetic, Toiletry, and Fragrance Association (CTFA) (www.ctfa.org)

Federal Citizen Information Center (FCIC) (www.pueblo.gsa.gov)

Just-Food.com (www.just-food.com)

ProductScan Online (www.productscan.com)

Product Web (www.productweb.com)

Key Consumer Products Companies by 2003 Revenue

Company	Revenue ($M)	1-Yr. Change (%)	Employees
Nestle	70,823	10	253,000
Unilever	53,674	10	234,000
Procter & Gamble	43,377	8	98,000
Johnson & Johnson	41,862	15	110,600
Philip Morris Int'l	33,389	17	40,000
Kraft Foods	31,010	4	106,000
PepsiCo	26,971	7	143,000
Tyson Foods	24,549	5	120,000
Coca-Cola Co.	21,044	8	49,000
ConAgra Foods	19,839	−28	63,000
Sara Lee Corp.	18,291	4	145,800
L'Oreal	17,609	18	50,500
Groupe Danone	16,508	16	88,607
Kimberly-Clark	14,348	6	62,000
Anheuser-Busch	14,147	4	23,316
Cadbury Schweppes	11,487	35	55,799
Colgate-Palmolive Co.	9,903	7	36,600
Gillette Co.	9,252	10	29,400
Kellogg Co.	8,812	6	25,250
H.J. Heinz Co.	8,237	−13	38,900

Sources: Hoover's; WetFeet analysis.

Energy and Utilities

Industry Overview

The industrial revolution started with the steam engine and still depends on energy produced from natural resources. The process begins when energy companies extract fossil fuels such as oil, coal, and natural gas from Mother Earth. These natural resources are turned into electricity and delivered to the consumer's door by power utilities companies, or they are processed into fuels, such as gasoline, propane, heating oil, or industrial coke for making steel. They are supplemented by water-powered hydroelectric generators and by uranium-powered nuclear generators. In any case, the result is the energy on which industrial countries are dependent. Without it we could not run our home appliances or our factories, travel by car or airplane, talk on the phone, or watch television.

Although extremely profitable, the industry has endured some upheavals: In early 1999, oil prices dropped below $10 per barrel—the lowest level since before the oil crises of the 1970s—due to a global petroleum surplus. While prices did recover, oil equipment and services companies took a particularly hard hit. Then, in 2001, rising energy prices caused power crises, especially in California—resulting in more regulatory attention being paid to energy companies. Also in 2001, high-flying energy broker Enron imploded in bankruptcy while its executive officers came under scrutiny for alleged shady dealings; the entire energy-trading sector has slowed as a result of this and other alleged corporate malfeasance. And then, in 2003, vast swaths of the eastern part of the United States and Canada lost their power after power-grid transmission lines in Ohio failed.

Conflicting forces will shape the future of the energy industry. Deregulation, initiated by the 1992 National Energy Policy Act, is transforming energy companies from regulated monopolies to free-market competitors, changing the face of the utilities industry. Continuing expansion of industrial development across the planet will spur increased global consumption of energy. However, that will cause worsening pollution and the depletion of natural resources, raising the question: Can we continue using energy as we have been? Perhaps not.

Some energy policies already foreshadow changes, an example being new, stringent EPA regulations in the United States. In the near term, though, neither environmental concerns nor volatile oil prices are likely to threaten the U.S. energy and utilities industry's role as a major supplier to the world market. It enjoys annual revenues of hundreds of billions of dollars and a demand that could double by 2020.

Trends

Terrorism and Political Unrest

9/11. Terrorist bombings in Indonesia and Saudi Arabia. The never-ending violence between Israel and Palestine. What it all adds up to for energy companies and utilities, is massive uncertainty. Will oil prices remain steady, allowing them to predict oil revenues (for oil companies) or costs (for utilities) and make business plans they are confident it? Or will some terrorist act suddenly cause oil prices to skyrocket? The energy and utilities industry, like the world in general, is a very uncertain place these days.

Electrical Power Capacity Problems

In August 2003, several power-grid transmission lines in Ohio failed, causing domino-like failures at electrical utilities across the eastern United States and Canada. The result: the Blackout of 2003. While blackouts can be fun for kids, who love the prospect of having dinner by candlelight, or for twenty-somethings who roamed city streets drinking on-the-house beverages handed out by local taverns, they're not fun for the economy. They mean lost revenue, lost wages, and so on. So this was big news for more reasons than the novelty of how cool it was to see, for once, the stars in the sky above Manhattan.

Some blamed the blackout on the privatization of energy and utility companies, saying that in the struggle to make profits they cut spending on areas that might have prevented this massive of a system failure. Whatever the case, it's clear that the system as it currently stands does not have the capacity for spikes in demand for power.

Playing Politics

The oil companies don't retain armies of lawyers and lobbyists—or make huge political contributions—for nothing. With strong ecological arguments existing against exploiting oil extraction in places like Alaska, the oil companies depend on legal and political clout to ensure they'll be able to continue exploiting oil finds. No example of the importance of political clout is better than Florida. The federal government recently agreed to purchase the rights to oil fields off the Gulf Coast of Florida from oil companies to prevent drilling there. Meanwhile, Halliburton, where Vice President Dick Cheney served as CEO before signing on with George W. Bush in his presidential campaign, received enormous contracts to help rebuild the oilfields of Iraq following the U.S. invasion in 2003—without even having to submit bids for the new work.

How It Breaks Down

America's energy companies are clustered in the Oil Patch region of Louisiana and East Texas, though many have major offices in Los Angeles and other coastal cities. The Big Oil companies are global; Exxon alone has a presence in some 100 countries. By contrast, utilities are generally more local in nature, usually doing business in a single city or region—though with deregulation, this is beginning to change. The vast industry can be broken down like this:

Integrated Oil and Natural Gas

We have John D. Rockefeller and his Standard Oil Company to thank for the vertical integration of the world's largest oil and energy companies. His empire has long since dispersed, but its legacy remains in the form of giants like Chevron, Exxon, and Phillips, which are involved in every phase of petroleum production and sales—from the extraction of crude oil through refining and shipping all the way up to the gas pump. Big Oil is a major force in the world's economy, but it is susceptible to global surpluses and plummeting oil prices when members of the Organization of Petroleum Exporting Countries (OPEC) cannot agree to restrain production.

Consumption and production of natural gas have grown far more rapidly in recent years partly due to its environmental advantage over oil. Also, natural gas is relatively less expensive as an electricity-generating fuel—an advantage that has been magnified by the competitive nature of the electricity industry since deregulation. While Big Oil is increasingly involved in the natural gas business, there are still specialists such as Questar Corporation.

Equipment and Service

Companies such as Schlumberger and Halliburton provide the equipment and services that make it possible for the oil, coal, and gas companies to extract those products from Mother Earth. This once-booming sector took a hard hit in the late '90s due to overproduction. While the largest companies will certainly survive, boutique concerns such as Dawson Geophysical (a technology expert) are more vulnerable.

Coal

Coal is primarily used for electricity generation and in a few manufacturing industries. It is increasingly in demand as developing countries such as China and India wire themselves for electricity. However, environmental concerns may put a damper on the use of coal. The 1990 Clean Air Act called for cuts in high-sulfur coal production, and there are growing worries about global warming caused by burning fossil fuels. Even if coal consumption continues at current levels, reserves will last only another 200 years. Despite these concerns, the near-term future of coal production and consumption should continue to be robust.

Utilities

More than 3,000 utilities in the United States deliver electric power to individual homes and businesses. Major players include the Southern Company (the nation's largest investor-owned utility) as well as regional giants such as Pacific Gas and Electric in California and Consolidated Edison in New York. The balance of the industry comprises federal agencies such as the Tennessee Valley Authority; local, publicly owned utilities, which are usually run by municipal or state agencies; and rural, nonprofit electric cooperatives, which serve small communities.

Nonutilities

Though they're in the business of electric power generation and distribution, nonutilities serve large individual clients—mostly utility companies that need extra electricity—as opposed to cities or regions. Though they only account for about 10 percent of power generation, nonutilities—such as Duke Energy— represent the fastest-growing sector of the industry. In the wake of deregulation, smaller-scale generators are freer to sell energy to big distributors, and small, efficient producers can be quite profitable.

Key Jobs for MBAs

Project Manager

For candidates who combine technical training with excellent business and communication skills, project management is the way to go. Stress levels can be high, but so are the pay and the sense of accomplishment that comes with the work. These jobs require at least a BS in engineering, as well as an MBA or an excellent industry track record.

Salary range: $80,000 to $200,000.

Marketer or Public Relations Specialist

Marketing people must have a solid understanding of the client's energy needs, and of the utility or energy company's ability to meet them. Once again, candidates who combine technical and marketing backgrounds have the edge.

Salary range: $30,000 to $150,000.

Trade Representative

Traditionally, people in these positions handled the sales of oil and other energy products in the futures markets. These days, electricity is becoming as much a commodity as oil; as a result, utilities now offer these types of positions as well. Candidates should have degrees in either engineering or business and marketing, plus proven negotiation or communication skills. People with both technology and MBA degrees can expect to do particularly well.

Salary range: $50,000 to $150,000.

Job Prospects

According to the Bureau of Labor Statistics, the number of jobs in the utilities sector is expected to grow very slowly in coming years. Even worse, the number of jobs in the oil and gas sector is projected to shrink between 2000 and 2010, at least in the United States. There are several reasons for this. The first is that the spate of recent mergers and acquisitions in both sectors has resulted in more than a few layoffs. The second is that technological advances have and will continue to result in productivity gains. Finally, most sources of petroleum in the United States are already tapped out.

At the same time, the number of jobs is projected to skyrocket in the water supply and sanitary services of the utilities sector, while the job outlook for folks like petroleum engineers and geoscientists looks good for those willing to work abroad.

In the energy sector, job seekers face a particularly unstable market as prices (and profits) fluctuate drastically. But don't throw away your geology or petroleum engineering degree yet; recruiters at Big Oil companies are anxious to hire qualified candidates. Entry-level jobs for engineers will be the most plentiful. Firms primarily recruit new engineers from the undergraduate level. Although fewer in number than engineering opportunities, entry-level business jobs should be available mainly in support roles such as accounting and human resources. Companies typically favor internal candidates who started as engineers to fill higher-level positions, but firms do recruit MBAs and some mid-career candidates, if in small proportions compared to the number of engineers in their ranks.

The deregulation of the utilities industry also means brand-new opportunities. With competition comes the need for expanded marketing, sales, communications, and PR departments. In addition, many utilities, suddenly free to diversify their business interests, have entered the telecommunications industry, with the

Southern Company and American Electric Power leading the way. Such seismic shifts in the industry are sure to open up new opportunities for young, ambitious employees, as formerly stuffy, hierarchical organizations are forced to entertain new ideas.

Additional Resources

American Gas Association (www.aga.org)

Center for Energy and Economic Development (www.ceednet.org)

Edison Electric Institute (www.eei.org)

Energy Crossroads (eetd.lbl.gov/EnergyCrossroads/EnergyCrossroads.html)

Energy Information Administration (www.eia.doe.gov)

Energy Science and Technology Virtual Library
(www.osti.gov/EnergyFiles)

Gas Technology Institute (www.gastechnology.org)

Oil and Gas Journal (ogj.pennnet.com/home.cfm)

Organization of the Petroleum Exporting Companies (OPEC) (www.opec.org)

U.S. Department of Energy (www.energy.gov)

Key Energy and Utility Companies by 2003 Revenue			
Company	Revenue ($M)	1-Yr. Change (%)	Employees
BP	232,571	30	103,700
Exxon Mobil	213,199	19	88,300
Royal Dutch/Shell Group	201,728	12	119,000
TOTAL	131,568	22	110,783
ChevronTexaco	112,937	23	50,582
ConocoPhillips	104,196	106	39,000
Valero Energy Corp.	37,969	41	19,621
Marathon Oil	36,678	17	27,007
Duke Energy	22,529	44	23,800
Halliburton Co.	16,246	30	101,000
Sunoco	15,867	27	14,900
Exelon	15,813	6	20,000
American Electric Power Co.	14,545	0	22,075
Amerada Hess Corp.	14,311	20	11,481
FirstEnergy	12,307	1	15,905
El Paso Corp.*	12,194	−79	11,855
Edison International	12,135	6	15,407
Dominion Resources	12,078	18	16,700
Southern Co.	11,251	7	25,762
TXU Corp.	11,008	10	14,235
PG&E	10,435	−17	20,600

*2002 figures.
Sources: Hoover's; WetFeet analysis.

Entertainment and Sports

Industry Overview

In entertainment and sports, the profits come from discretionary spending, so these industries enjoy the most success in economically stable countries where leisure dollars flow freely. Industry companies supply their audiences with large-scale sporting events, music concerts, sit-coms, and silver-screen masterpieces. Simply put, they're in the business of fun.

Even during economically depressed periods, this industry flourishes as an escape from hard times—for all walks of life. And standing at the pinnacle of entertainment culture are the celebrities: the movie stars, quarterbacks, rock stars, talk-show hosts who seem to realize our dreams and thereby give us hope. This is the only industry whose product is an illusion—neither a good nor a service, and yet both at the same time.

The culture in this industry is one of anticorporate, studied casualness. There are still uniforms—an ever-changing array of baseball caps and jackets in the music business, for example. But they're invariably less starchy, more expressive of individualism, than anything worn to work in the fields of finance or law. The people? Well, there's no people like show people, and the sports world has even more pep. This is a high-energy crowd. It's also a big-ego crowd, and working with its members can be both stimulating and frustrating.

Bottom line, though, is that even if your job does not bring you into contact with the creative members of the industry, the glamour rubs off, lending an aura of excitement to mundane tasks that would be boring in any other industry. Poring over Nielsen ratings all day doesn't sound so bad when you describe it to your dinner companions as analyzing the relative sex appeal of Jerry Springer, Oprah Winfrey, and Dan Rather.

Trends

Television

Although broadcast networks still yield the highest ratings and generate more revenue than ever before, high programming costs are cutting into profits, and lower-overhead cable channels and networks are threatening to overturn broadcasting's dominance. The broadcast networks' parent companies are responding to these challenges by hiring people who can boost ad sales and cut costs. "Reality" programming is another way broadcasters are trying to lower expenses; it's much cheaper to have a couple of cameras follow nonactors around all day, even in some exotic location, than to pay big salaries to talent and produce the usual sitcom or prime-time drama.

Music

Though the television industry must contend with the commercial-skipping TiVo, and the movie industry has concerns about DVD piracy in Asia and Latin America, no industry is more paranoid about a technological advance eating into its profits than the music industry is about file sharing. With music sales down 20 percent since 2000, the major labels are in big trouble. Though other factors (e.g., a perceived lack of compelling artists, artificially high CD prices, competition from "higher-value" DVDs, and the soft economy) are involved, file sharing has clearly had a negative impact on album sales. The only bright spot is Apple's iTunes digital distribution website, which has enjoyed early success selling music files owned by the majors.

Sports

Over the past 20 or 30 years, the major trend in sports has been the tremendous growth in revenues, primed by televised broadcasting of games. This innovation led first to increased advertising sales, then to sponsorships, and then to stadium naming rights. Player endorsements provide a human (or superhuman) face to these sports-marketing efforts. Over time, teams and leagues have become much more business-minded, and revenues have increased many times over. This transformation has fueled the need for business people to wheel and deal, and squeeze as much money out of every sporting event or deal as possible.

How It Breaks Down

Entertainment

As we move into the digital age, it's getting more difficult to cleanly break down the industry into traditional categories. One reason for this is the proliferation of new forms of entertainment—CD-ROMs, the Internet, and the like. Another reason is that many film, television, and music companies have united to form entertainment conglomerates.

While the landscape of the industry is changing, for the purposes of this profile we break entertainment into three traditional categories: television, film, and music, and then follow these up with a look at sports entertainment as its own standalone category.

Television. Television is arguably the 20th century's most significant—and most popular—technological development. In 1945, there were fewer than 7,000 television sets in use in the United States. Today, almost every American household has a television, and two out of three households have more than one. The number of channels and networks—and number of jobs in television—has grown along with television's popularity. But competition for jobs in this segment of the entertainment industry remains particularly stiff. At the entry level, this translates into poor compensation. And although executives are paid generously, job security is always an issue in television. Most opportunities are in Los Angeles and New York, where the networks and major production companies are headquartered.

Film. Before there was a television in every home, film was the medium that created a common national language. Taking weekend trips to the movie house to view double and triple features, and the newsreels that ran between each film was a way of life for people in the '30s, '40s, and '50s. But television soon replaced the movies as the most popular entertainment medium. The movie industry for the most part remained stagnant until the release of *Jaws* in 1975. That film's gross revenue—more than $260 million domestically—and sensational special effects reinvigorated and redefined the film industry. Film studios rushed to make blockbusters, which cost millions of dollars to produce but when successful could return more than $100 million in box-office grosses.

Music. Technically, the recording industry got its start when Emile Berliner invented a prototype phonograph that recorded music. But the business of music really took off with the large-scale launch of a new technology—when radio stations started broadcasting in the '20s.

Today the industry is dominated by large corporate music groups such as Warner Music Group, Universal, and BMG. These companies produce most of the music in your local CD store's racks and tend to take advantage of—either through acquisition or pressing and distribution deals—any upstart labels that do particularly well in the marketplace. The most recent round of consolidation in the music industry brought independent labels in "outsider" genres such as rap and alternative rock into the major-label fold.

Sports

The Big Four. At the professional level, the Big Four spectator sports (baseball, basketball, football, and hockey) are the giants in terms of fan interest, media attention, and revenue. Over the years, these sports have evolved so that each now has one dominant governing body (Major League Baseball, The National Basketball Association, The National Football League, and The National Hockey League) reigning supreme. Originally, the main functions of the governing bodies were to create and enforce rules and policies governing owners, players, and referees; to impartially organize games between teams; and to maintain statistics and issue awards to winning teams and outstanding players. While those functions remain, the incredible growth of sports as a revenue engine has propelled the governing bodies to become full-fledged businesses that encompass marketing and PR, logo licensing, television rights licensing, and revenue distribution among teams.

Team owners tend to be either wealthy individuals or entertainment companies. Owners hire and fire players in accordance to rules hammered out by the governing bodies and the players' associations and are responsible for all marketing related to their teams, as well as income streams such as ticket and concession sales, advertising, and merchandising.

The Big Four also own and operate minor league teams, which have their own governing bodies. Just like the collegiate teams do, minor league teams provide many professionals with their entrée into the industry.

Sports management. The realization that companies would pay to be associated with the personality and achievements of pro golfer Arnold Palmer—and thereby increase their brand value—led his friend and financial manager Mark H. McCormack to almost single-handedly create the field of sports management, and the sports powerhouse IMG with it, in 1960. A talent agent in the entertainment industry usually focuses on finding lucrative projects for his or her clients and then negotiating the best possible deal, but the sports agent (or sports manager) will often take the process one step further. Naturally, he or she will solicit or review offers from teams and negotiate contracts, but the real money is made off of the court (or field, or ice), in the form of endorsements.

At the top of the heap are integrated sports marketing and management companies like IMG. Big advertising companies have sought to diversify by either creating sports management companies, as Interpublic did with Octagon, or purchasing them outright, as Clear Channel did with SFX Sports Group. Traditional talent agencies such as The William Morris Agency also have sports practices. These agencies represent the biggest, most recognizable athletes in a wide range of sports.

It should be no surprise that most people who enter this field are tax or contract lawyers, certified public accountants, or personal finance managers; basically, people who are comfortable with contracts, numbers, large sums of money, and the law. Some states require registration to help protect college athletes from getting taken advantage of; most professional players' associations offer agent certification to do the same for their members.

Sports marketing. Sports marketing is a rather nebulous term for a number of activities in the sports world; pretty much every element of the sports industry is involved in marketing in one way or another. The powerhouses are the integrated sports management and marketing companies discussed above.

At the league level, sports marketers help companies market various consumer goods and services by allowing their logos, events, and players to be tied to marketing and advertising campaigns. In addition to direct revenue, there is also an extended benefit when the goods and services being marketed fit in well with a league's image. At the team level, sports marketers help the sales staff sell tickets and corporate sponsorships by building interest in the team through promotions, advertising, and game-day events that complement the game itself. They also help place the team name and logo on a variety of products—everything from caps to Coke cans—to maximize merchandising and sponsorship revenues and maintain a connection with fans. Public relations departments work with the media to get valuable coverage for games, players, promotional efforts, and human-interest stories, all of which enhance the team's appeal to fans and, by extension, to corporate sponsors.

On the other side of the fence sit companies that want to reach sports fans. Nike and Gatorade are far and away the sports-product companies that most actively market to sports fans, but the appeal of sports is so broad that beer companies such as Anheuser-Busch, automakers such as Ford, credit card companies such as VISA, and telecommunications companies such as AT&T are among the largest advertisers of televised sports events. The biggest advertisers have dedicated sports marketing departments that find suitable advertising, promotional, and sponsorship efforts that will reach targeted consumers and, short term, turn them into customers, while over the long term enhance the company's or product's brand.

Key Job for MBAs

Marketing and Promotion

These are perhaps the most transferable of all skill sets in this business. Vast and constant infusions of market analysis, research, writing, graphics, and well-organized planning and distribution support every important sports event, hit song, new television show, and box-office gamble. Being an account executive or marketing manager is also great training for whatever senior executive role you may ultimately want to play in one of these entertainment engines. The gas they all run on is marketing and promotion. Learn how to do it effectively and well and you'll always have work.

Salary range: $40,000 to $110,000.

Job Prospects

Keep in mind that this could be the most competitive industry out there. Getting a job in sports or entertainment is a difficult undertaking that requires persistence, intense networking, and good luck. Every year, hundreds upon thousands of job seekers flood New York and Los Angeles hoping to become celebrities, and the majority of them wind up waiting tables to make ends meet. And, if they decide to stay in show biz, they eventually end up taking jobs in production or administration. Take heart in the fact, though, that companies can't ignore talent. If you prove that you've got the skills to thrive in a challenging and nontraditional work environment, then you're in for a thrilling ride.

Careers in this industry usually start at the entry level; agents, personal managers, and studio executives usually got their start as lowly assistants. Once launched on their careers, people in the entertainment industry tend to change jobs frequently, and contacts in the industry are crucial.

For those of you with a business or technical background, work is more readily available. The big corporations that dominate the industry always need people in the standard management functions such as finance, HR, IT, marketing, and communications. Technicians are needed in traditional fields such as sound engineering and photography, and in the rapidly expanding fields of digital special effects: Dozens or perhaps hundreds of companies in Southern California and the San Francisco Bay Area employ software engineers and other specialists to create digital special effects, which are at the center of films like *The Matrix*, *Monsters Inc.*, *Lord of the Rings*, and *Spider-Man*, and contribute unobtrusively to scores of other films, removing unwanted telephone cables from outdoor scenes and wrinkles from stars' faces. Leading companies in this field include Pixar, PDI, Sony Pictures Imageworks, and Industrial Light and Magic.

Key Entertainment Companies by 2003 Revenue

Company	Revenue ($M)	1-Yr. Change (%)	Employees
Time Warner	38,076	−7	80,000
Walt Disney	27,061	7	112,000
Viacom	26,585	8	117,750
Sony Corp. of America	23,544	27	22,000
Bertelsmann	21,089	10	73,221
News Corp. Ltd.	20,096	23	37,000
Fox Entertainment	11,002	13	12,900
ABC	10,941	12	n/a
Clear Channel	8,931	6	36,500
CBS	7,761	4	n/a
NBC	6,871	−4	n/a
Universal Studios	6,622	1	22,146
InterActiveCorp	6,328	37	25,700
EMI Group	3,424	−2	8,088
BMG Entertainment	3,404	20	4,880
Metro-Goldwyn-Mayer	1,883	14	1,280
DreamWorks SKG*	1,813	−18	1,600
AMC Entertainment	1,792	34	18,300
Loews Cineplex	1,772	107	16,500
LucasFilm	1,200	−11	1,800

*2002 figures.
Sources: Hoover's; WetFeet analysis.

Additional Resources

Billboard (www.billboard.com)

EntertainmentCareers.net (www.entertainmentcareers.net)

Hollywood Reporter (www.hollywoodreporter.com)

McKinsey Quarterly: Media and Entertainment
(www.mckinseyquarterly.com/category_editor.asp?L2=17)

Work in Sports (www.workinsports.com/home.asp)

Health Care

Industry Overview

Although this line of work probably interests you because of its humanitarian and service aspects, the industry as a whole—hospitals, nursing homes, home health care, specialized clinics, and nontraditional options such as homeopathic treatment—is all business these days. And a big business it is: The United States spends more than a trillion dollars a year on health care.

The health care industry provides diagnostic, healing, rehabilitation, and prevention services for the injured, ailing, incapacitated, and disabled. The individual physician is its first line of contact with consumers. However, the health care organization—the hospital or health management organization (HMO)—is the conduit of insurance payments, which form the preponderance of the industry's, and the physician's, revenues. The lion's share of these revenues comes from employee health insurance plans, Medicare (health insurance for Americans over the age of 65), and Medicaid (health insurance for Americans on welfare). Health care organizations, except for county hospitals, are usually run for profit. This creates tension between doctors who want to prescribe expensive treatments and diagnostic tests and health care organizations, which want to cut costs.

There is an abundance of opportunities for people interested in health care—whether or not you have an MD (or even a bachelor's degree). People are living longer and needing more preventative and long-term care. The demand for health care workers is expected to grow faster than the average rate of increase for all other occupations between 2000 and 2010. There's a growing need for home care aides, registered nurses, physician assistants, nurse practitioners, physical therapists, nontraditional health aides, and physicians. Not to mention all of the technical and administrative jobs that are in high demand as hospitals focus their energies on efficient management and profitability.

Trends

Runaway Costs

Doctors and hospitals have been dealing with rising costs for a long time—and each year the situation seems to get worse. Malpractice insurance premiums, soaring prescription-drug prices, the increasing numbers of uninsured Americans, rising salaries for nurses and other support staff: All these things mean higher costs for caregivers. At the same time, revenues for doctors and hospitals are falling, as insurers are doing everything in their power to lower claims payments.

Meanwhile, the insurers are not feeling the squeeze nearly as much as the caregivers. The reason: They make sure that revenues from premiums rise at a higher rate than claims payments.

The Uninsured Nation

Currently there are 43 million Americans without health insurance. That's an awful lot of people. And the number of uninsured Americans is sure to rise. Why? Insurance premiums continue to skyrocket. The reason for this is all the consolidation among health insurers. Most recently, Anthem announced its acquisition of WellPoint Health Networks, and UnitedHealth Group announced plans to acquire Mid Atlantic Medical Services. The result of all this M&A activity is less competition among health insurers—and higher premiums. Indeed, employers are facing double-digit percentage increases in health premium costs each year. Meaning more and more of the cost of health insurance is being passed on to employees—and more and more people can't afford health care coverage.

How It Breaks Down

Hospitals

Despite the increased outsourcing of medical records, housekeeping, lab testing, and clinical services such as orthopedics and radiology, hospitals are still the biggest employers in the health care industry. The huge networks such as HCA and Tenet need a steady supply of doctors, nurses, administrators, medical technicians, therapists, and other support staff. In areas where competition from HMOs is mounting and cost cutting is a priority, former staff may move outside the immediate confines of a hospital. However, close and important links remain—particularly for any type of surgery or specialized treatment such as chemotherapy.

HMOs and PPOs

Health maintenance organizations and preferred provider organizations are hybrids between a hospital and an insurance company. Each type of managed care plan covers primary care visits, preventative services, and copayments for prescription drugs, while only PPOs allow the enrollee to choose his or her physician (HMOs maintain a list of plan-approved doctors). Some of the largest organizations actually have their own medical staffs and facilities at which they treat patients; smaller ones may just access networks of private providers and hospitals. Competition is fierce in this arena—mergers, acquisitions, and internal strife often destabilize the job market. Coventry, Humana, Harvard Pilgrim Health Care, Group Health Cooperative, and Pacificare (one of the leading Medicare HMOs) are a few of the better-known players.

Specialty Providers

As hospitals have attempted to cut costs, they have turned to firms that can provide specialized services at rock-bottom prices. These include everything from nursing homes (Beverly Enterprises) to home infusion therapy providers (Apria Healthcare) to diabetes treatment providers (American Healthways).

Clinics that focus on special treatments such as chemotherapy, MRI and other scanning techniques, and physical therapy for the handicapped are also proliferating. Most are small and locally run, but Gambro and Fresenius Medical Care are two enormous service companies that focus on this type of care; more will undoubtedly emerge as their popularity increases.

Home Care

Advances in technology have done much to improve efficiency and reduce costs for both patients and home care staff. Today, home care nurses and aides can administer complex treatments, previously only available in hospitals or clinics, to the elderly and severely disabled in their own homes. And because almost all hospitals and HMOs now release patients before they are self-sufficient, home care is often the most viable choice. Most jobs in this sector don't require much training (they are closely supervised by an RN, NP, or physician), just deep reserves of patience and kindness. But the pay is low—often under $10 an hour—and the work is arduous. The rewards? Hours are extremely flexible, and there is plenty of personal contact with clients.

Key Job for MBAs

Health Care Managers

These are the jobs where an MBA comes in handy and a background in cost cutting, marketing, and information management will give you an edge over the competition. Lots of people want these jobs, and though industry observers predict that the number of managerial slots in hospitals and HMOs will shrink to perhaps half the current number, the need for qualified executive staff in home health care, nursing homes, and clinics is expected to more than make up the difference.

Salary range: $55,000 and up. Experienced managers with an impressive track record in meeting and maintaining strict budgets can earn well into the six-figure range.

Job Prospects

There are several types of health care professionals requiring varying levels of education and training. Registered nurses (RNs) are trained at the undergraduate level, whereas nurse practitioners (NPs) have received a master's-level training. To qualify for some positions (including doctor, nurse, tech), you need technical training, and to land a job you often need a strong network in a given area and practical experience in the industry.

RNs, pharmacists, and radiological technicians are currently in very high demand, and they will continue to be in demand in the coming years. Why? The population is growing; the numbers of elderly in the United States are growing; and health care spending is being cut wherever possible—which means that whenever a nurse can do something a doctor may have done in the past, that's exactly what's going to happen. Employers are looking at ways to attract people to these in-demand professions by offering signing bonuses, tuition reimbursement or loan repayment, flexible scheduling, and incentives for voluntary overtime shifts.

Opportunities will also grow at a strong clip in many other health care functions, from doctor, physician assistant, and optometrist to occupational therapist, audiologist, and physical therapist to home health aide, medical record technologist, and speech pathologist.

Hospitals and HMOs offers jobs in management as well as medicine—particularly if you understand IT and data system development. As a job seeker, you should know that HMOs have been the catalyst for many of the efficient business practices imposed on all aspects of health care in recent years. Technical and administrative support positions are in high demand as the health care industry evolves in a competitive market. Health care IT is a steadily growing sector, due to the industry's relative lack of IT investment thus far.

Key Health Care Organizations by 2003 Revenue			
Company	Revenue ($M)	1-Yr. Change (%)	Employees
Blue Cross and Blue Shield*	162,800	14	150,000
McKesson	57,121	14	24,500
Cardinal Health	50,467	−1	50,000
AmerisourceBergen	49,657	10	14,800
UnitedHealth Group	28,823	15	33,000
Kaiser Permanente	25,300	12	147,000
HCA	21,808	11	242,000
WellPoint Health Networks	20,360	17	19,100
Cigna	18,808	−3	32,700
Aetna	17,976	−10	27,600
Anthem	16,771	26	20,130
AdvancePCS	14,111	8	6,500
Express Scripts	13,295	8	8,575
Tenet Healthcare Corp.	13,212	51	109,759
Humana	12,226	9	13,700
Health Net	11,065	9	9,053
PacifiCare Health System	11,009	−1	7,700
Caremark Rx	9,067	33	4,870
Baxter International	8,916	10	51,300
Medtronic	7,665	20	30,000

*2002 figures.
Sources: Hoover's; WetFeet analysis.

Additional Resources

Agency for Healthcare Research and Quality (www.ahcpr.gov)

InPharm.com (www.inpharm.com)

Knowledge @ Wharton: Health Economics
(knowledge.wharton.upenn.edu/category.cfm?catid=6)

McKinsey Quarterly: Health Care
(www.mckinseyquarterly.com/category_editor.asp?L2=12)

Internet and New Media

Industry Overview

Trying ardently to fulfill the promise of the Web, Internet companies—start-ups as well as online extensions of bricks-and-mortar companies—have singled out some activity to reinvent by conducting it on the Internet—distributing textbooks, software, or greeting cards; disseminating medical information, fiction, or law school classes; planning parties; or swapping vacation homes. For all of these activities, and many more, the Internet makes it possible to distribute information of all kinds and conduct a transaction at the same time, anywhere in the world, immediately.

In the process, companies are doing a stunningly wide variety of things online—selling products, producing newspaper- and magazine-style publications, providing services like travel agencies and stock brokerages, delivering search engines, recruiting employees, building brands, and developing online gaming networks, to name a few. Add to this all of the companies that underpin and service these endeavors—the online ad agencies, Internet service providers (ISPs), and management consultancies—and you get a sense of just how broad this industry is.

In recent years, Internet companies have witnessed a precipitous decline in advertising revenue. As a result, many pure-play Internet companies have gone under, and some old-economy companies decided to scale back their Web operations, leaving tens of thousands of people out of work. In the new world order, Internet companies must demonstrate profitability or a clear plan for it, or risk near-term financial disaster. In other words, to make it on the Web these days, you'd better have a strong e-commerce component, or at least a viable subscription model if you're primarily a content provider.

In the case of public Internet companies, the majority have disappointed stake-holders with lower revenues and longer-than-projected paths to profitability. As far as the remaining private start-up shops are concerned, most are very short on cash; the much-needed venture capital funding no longer flows freely. The result: Companies fold, get acquired, or scale back considerably.

Trends

Net Taxes?

Internet taxation has been an issue for a number of years. Should Internet service providers or e-commerce operations have to collect sales taxes? The argument against online taxes has long been the complexity of how to apply those taxes. Do you charge the sales tax rate in the state where the ISP or e-tailer is located? Do you tax at the rate charged by the consumer's state? A moratorium on Internet taxes imposed by the U.S. Congress recently expired, putting this issue on the front burner once again. It's backed by traditional retailers, who don't like the rising competition from e-commerce sites, which are registering higher revenues every year, as well as by states which feel they're losing out on funds they're legally due—and which, in this era of government budget shortfalls, they desperately need.

A New Boom?

The dot-com boom ended when advertisers stopped pouring money into advertising on the Web, and online advertising revenues suddenly dried up. Recently, though, advertising revenues have begun to pick up again. One driver of this trend has been sales of ad space to companies who want their sites to show up on results pages for searches on certain words or phrases—so-called keywords. Things are looking so good that Google, the most popular search engine in the industry, is set to go public this year, with some saying its IPO could value it at $20 billion or more.

But don't go thinking this signals a return to the go-go days of the 1990s. For one thing, there aren't many other companies that look like viable IPO candidates aside from Google. For another, venture funding for Internet companies isn't growing on trees these days, as it seemed to be 5 years ago. And finally, many companies are pressuring search engines to prevent advertisers from using keywords whose trademarks belong to them and their brands—meaning a potential slowdown in online advertising revenue.

The Bright Spots

The Internet seems to work best, from a business perspective, for companies engaged in low-overhead e-commerce—for instance, financial, software, and travel-services sites that don't store or ship inventory have low costs once they've established their technological infrastructure. For example, Expedia, a leading travel site, operates on a 70 percent profit margin. Amazon.com, on the other hand—which has to deal with procuring and shipping actual physical products—operates at a margin of about 25 percent.

How It Breaks Down

The industry is a baggy monster that resists classification. The following breakdown is not a definitive taxonomy but rather a chance for the uninitiated to make some sense of a rapidly changing landscape.

Publishers

Online publications make money by selling advertising or subscriptions or both. Most of the players are losing money, and widespread profitability seems unlikely in the near future. Many players in this field are online ventures of already-established media brands. Some examples include the *Wall Street Journal Interactive Edition*, a subscription-based version of the leading business newspaper, and ESPN.com, an extension of the sports cable channel.

There are also a number of important players whose primary presence is online. A few examples are CNet, which provides news and information on the online world, and CitySearch, which is actually a cluster of publications, each devoted to life (restaurants, movies, community-service opportunities, etc.) in a given city. And hundreds of daily newspapers put all or part of their content on websites that are still exploring the differences between reporting for print and for the Web.

Vendors

Vendors make money by selling goods or services. The best-known online seller of goods is Amazon.com. Mail-order companies with websites—Lands' End, for example—fall into this category. Other sellers provide services: E-Trade and Charles Schwab act as stockbrokers, Expedia acts as a travel agent, and FreeMarkets creates customized business-to-business online auctions for large buyers of industrial parts, raw materials, and commodities.

Aggregators and Portals

Some of the busiest sites on the Web fall into this category. Search engines—which account for five of the ten busiest websites—are aggregators (so named because they offer a huge aggregation of links to other websites). Portals (also known as *gateways* or *start pages*) are sites that serve as home base for Web surfers. The home page of AOL, for example, is designed as an Internet portal. In a move that typifies the fluidity and opportunism of this industry, the leading search engines, such as Yahoo!, have positioned themselves as gateways, and vice versa. Other so-called freestanding search engines such as the popular Google.com have opted for search performance over the glitz and glam of gateways.

All of these sites make money from banner advertising (think billboards on your computer screen) or, increasingly, through alliances with companies that pay a lot of money to be the gateway or aggregator's "preferred provider" of travel services, greeting cards, and so on.

Communities

Online communities serve as centers for people who share special interests. GeoCities is one of the largest, hosting a number of communities with interests as varied as fashion, golf, and government. Other examples of community sites include Motley Fool for small investors; BabyCenter, a site for parents; iVillage, a site for women; and PlanetOut, a site for gays and lesbians. All of these sites encourage users to sign up for free memberships by offering access to chat rooms, newsletters, and bulletin boards; some offer members the opportunity to construct Web pages, which then reside on the community site and serve as a draw for more members. Like many other Internet concerns, these sites used to make money primarily from advertising and alliances, but they are now trying to pump up revenue streams such as e-commerce and subscriptions.

Consulting and Support

This category encompasses all of the companies that have sprung up to support and provide services to the industry. The ISP (Internet service provider) world has consolidated quite a bit in recent years, with many smaller companies being bought and consolidated into national companies. Most of the major phone companies are also competing as ISPs. Local and long distance carriers such as SBC and AT&T provide the latest in DSL and high-speed cable Internet connections.

This segment also includes a variety of now-struggling consulting firms (and struggling units in bigger consulting firms with a variety of practices) that help develop websites, providing services such as management and strategic consulting specialized for Web companies, online advertising, e-commerce development, user-interface design, and, increasingly, all of the above.

Key Jobs for MBAs

Project Manager

The project manager (a.k.a. producer or product manager) acts to make sure that the various pieces of a multimedia puzzle—a website or a CD-ROM—are on track. This means making sure that the creative, technical, and business people are all in synch. Or as one job listing puts it, the producer "manages product from concept to final release, maintains product vision, and upholds business objectives." A project manager usually has substantial experience on the business or design side of things.

Salary range: $60,000 to $100,000.

Marketing Associate or Director

In these positions, you'll conceive and execute advertising campaigns in the virtual and physical worlds. You'll also build a site's brand. Titles vary quite a bit in marketing, but the general idea is to drive people to a company's website, and then make money by selling products or subscriptions or whatever else the site sells. Good communication skills are critical. Any previous marketing experience is helpful.

Salary range: $30,000 to $90,000.

Business Development

Alliances and partnerships between and among sites are one of the driving features of online business. Business development folks identify possible partners, then negotiate and close deals and maintain relationships. MBAs tend to fit well in business development.

Salary range: $40,000 to $120,000.

Job Prospects

Just 5 years ago, there were tons of thriving, vibrant Internet start-ups making their way up in the business world—and hiring tons of job seekers in the process. Then the bubble burst. Most of those start-ups have disappeared, and even those that haven't have cut back on staff. Indeed, Internet job openings have been few and far between in recent years, and sky-high demand among the laid off for those jobs meant they would be snapped up with lightning speed. Today, the Internet industry has matured—no more foosball tables and free lunches, and no more ignoring the bottom line. Although jobs are available, they're not available in large numbers, as was the case until 5 years ago—and job growth in this industry is not expected to be very strong in coming years. There's some demand for new hires in business development, marketing, content production, and operations, but not very much, and that's likely to continue to be the case.

Likewise, programmers in the industry are going to face only average job growth in their field in coming years. For one thing, a lot of software can now write simple code itself, eliminating some need for programmers. Also, more and more programming and other IT work is and will continue to be farmed out to cheaper overseas workers in coming years.

On the other hand, Internet companies continue to have strong need for good database administrators, software engineers, and other techies, and that need is only going to grow as systems get bigger and more complex.

Key Internet and New Media Companies by 2003 Revenue			
Company	**Revenue ($M)**	**1-Yr. Change (%)**	**Employees**
Microsoft Corp.	32,187	13.5	55,000
America Online	6,428	−10.1	18,000
Amazon.com	5,264	33.8	7,800
Charles Schwab Corp.	4,328	3.4	16,300
E-Trade Financial Corp.	2,179	14.1	3,500
eBay	2,165	78.3	6,200
Yahoo!	1,625	70.5	5,500
EarthLink	1,402	3.3	3,335
Google	962	176.5	1,628
Priceline.com	864	−13.9	293
CMP Media LLC	796	19.1	3,376
Ticketmaster	743	−8.4	n/a
Ameritrade Holding Corp.	731	65.0	1,732
Terra Lycos, S.A.	687	5.2	n/a
Monster Worldwide	680	−39.0	4,300
Expedia*	591	266.4	1,758
Travelocity.com	308	2.2	n/a
CNET Networks	246	3.9	1,700
Orbitz	242	37.8	308
Scottrade	223	32.0	1,000

*2002 figures.
Sources: Hoover's; WetFeet analysis.

Additional Resources

Internet.com (www.internet.com)

Red Herring (www.redherring.com)

The Industry Standard (www.thestandard.com)

Wired News (www.wired.com)

Investment Banking

Industry Overview

Investment banks are experts at calculating what a business is worth, usually for one of two purposes: to price a securities offering or to set the value of a merger or acquisition. Securities include stocks and bonds, and a stock offering may be an initial public offering (IPO) or any subsequent (or *secondary*) offering. In both cases, I-banks charge hefty fees for providing this valuation service, along with other kinds of financial and business advice.

When banks underwrite stock or bond issues, they ensure that institutional investors, such as mutual funds or pension funds, commit to purchasing the issue of stocks or bonds before it actually hits the market. In this sense, I-banks are intermediaries between the issuers of securities and the investing public. I-banks make markets to facilitate securities trading by buying and selling securities out of their own account and profiting from the spread between the bid and the ask price. In addition, many I-banks offer retail brokerage (retail meaning the customers are individual investors rather than institutional investors) and asset management services.

Not surprisingly, the center of this industry rests in the lofty aeries above Wall Street and Midtown in New York City. Other hot spots include London, San Francisco, and Silicon Valley. Firms also compete in Frankfurt, Tokyo, Hong Kong, and other foreign markets 24 hours a day.

Trends

Cool Down

As the global economic climate cools down, so has investment banking. IPO and M&A activity has all but dried up; the only bright spots on the Street are areas in which lower interest rates drive business, such as mortgage-backed and municipal securities. Meanwhile, the big banks have found themselves tremendously overstaffed, having hired new employees like gangbusters in the boom years of the 1990s. As a result, in the past couple of years, investment banks have laid off tens of thousands of employees. Reports vary, but some say employment levels are 25 percent lower than they were at their peak. At the same time, I-banking bonuses, which can comprise half or more of some employees' total annual compensation, have fallen by 50 percent or more. I-banks have also pulled back on college and MBA recruiting—but, because it's cheaper to employ a recent grad than someone with more experience, there are still jobs to be had for the cream of the crop from the best schools. More than ever, though, those who do I-banking internships will have the best shot at full-time openings.

Industry Consolidation

Investment banking has witnessed a rash of cross-industry mergers and acquisitions in recent times, largely due to the late-1999 repeal of the Depression-era Glass-Steagall Act. The repeal, which marked the deregulation of the financial services industry, now allows commercial banks, investment banks, insurers, and securities brokerages to offer one another's services. As I-banks add retail brokerage and lending to their offerings and commercial banks try to build up their investment banking services, the industry is undergoing some serious global consolidation, allowing clients to invest, save, and protect their money all under one roof. These mergers have only added to the downward pressure on employment in the industry, as merged institutions make an effort to reduce redundancy.

Among the M&A activity in recent years: First Boston and Donaldson, Lufkin & Jenrette were both acquired by Credit Suisse; J.P. Morgan and Hambrecht & Quist were swallowed by Chase; Robertson Stephens was acquired by FleetBoston; and Alex. Brown was acquired by Deutsche Bank.

Meanwhile, foreign firms like Deutsche Bank and UBS are moving into U.S. markets aggressively. The result: Firms in the United States and abroad are looking for partners or acquisitions to beef up their global presence. "Almost everything we do now has some cross-border component. More than 50 percent of my work is in foreign investments," says one insider. "Every day I see a wire come across about something going on somewhere like Kenya or India."

Scandals on the Street

The swing in the markets from up, up, up to down, down, down has focused a lot of scrutiny on firms on the Street. The biggest issue so far has been the fact that banks overrated the investment potential of client companies' stocks intentionally, deceiving investors in the pursuit of favorable relationships—and ongoing banking revenue opportunities—with those companies. Firms have also come under fire for the methods by which they allocated stock offerings (specifically, for whether they charged excessive commissions to clients who wanted to purchase hot offerings), as well as for possible manipulation of accounting rules in the course of presenting clients' financial info to potential investors.

To date, firms including Merrill Lynch, Credit Suisse First Boston, Citigroup, Goldman Sachs, Deutsche Bank, Bear Stearns, Morgan Stanley, J.P. Morgan Chase, and UBS—in other words, everybody who's anybody on the Street— have paid fines totaling in the billions of dollars to settle allegations against them, and the scrutiny of regulators remains sharp, with more fines sure to come. In addition, big-time players on the Street, including research analysts like Henry Blodget (Merrill Lynch) and Jack Grubman (Citigroup) and bankers like Frank Quattrone (CSFB) have been accused of misdeeds and/or fined and fired. However, it's important to realize that to behemoth institutions like the bulge-bracket banks, these fines are a drop in the bucket when compared to their total annual revenues. After all, regulators don't want to destroy the big banks; they're too central to the global economy. Whether the slap-on-the-wrist approach will result in permanent changes to the way banks do business remains to be seen.

New Relationships Between Research and Banking

All that said, several changes in the way banks do business seem sure, all of them relating to research: less of a link between research analysts' compensation and firms' banking revenues, less of a role for research analysts in seeking banking business, and more objectivity in research reports. Already, banks are enforcing new degrees of separation between bankers and research analysts: As part of a settlement with New York, Merrill Lynch agreed to strengthen the barriers between research and banking; and Citigroup has floated the idea of spinning off its research department into a distinct company. The SEC is now requiring research analysts to affirm in writing that the recommendations in their reports are truly what they believe, and that they have received no payment for specific research opinions (a requirement designed to de-link research analysts' compensation from their firms' banking efforts).

The tricky thing about all this is that separating research from banking makes it harder for banks to justify the costs of conducting research. Without revenues that are directly or indirectly the result of their research departments, research becomes purely a cost center. As a result, banks are likely to look to cut costs in research moving forward. That means research departments will either have to cover fewer companies or cover a greater number of companies per analyst—or both. Indeed, in the spring of 2003, Citigroup announced that it was ending its coverage of 117 companies and that it will eventually cover more companies with fewer analysts.

How It Breaks Down

The Bulge Bracket

There's no clear and uniformly accepted definition of this group, but it basically includes the biggest of the full-service investment banks. This is the group that matters most in investment banking, and their names confer distinction, whether you're a start-up with an IPO to sell, a Fortune 500 company planning an acquisition, or a job seeker sending out resumes. Merrill Lynch, Morgan Stanley, Goldman Sachs, Citigroup, Lehman Brothers, Credit Suisse First Boston, Deutsche Bank, and J. P. Morgan Chase hold top spots in this bracket, at least for the moment. A whole host of others fall into the second tier of major players, including Bear Stearns and UBS Investment Bank.

Boutiques and Regional Firms

Obviously, the investment banking world extends beyond New York and the bulge bracket, but the list of small firms is getting smaller as the market consolidates. The strongest boutique firms—Hambrecht & Quist, Montgomery Securities, and Alex. Brown—have all been acquired by commercial banks. But that's not to say independent firms are nearing extinction. The equity markets are strong, and that means big business for niche firms focusing on technology, biotechnology, and other high-growth industries. In New York, Allen & Co. and Lazard Frères still do big business in specialized fields. Volpe Brown Whelan and Thomas Weisel are Silicon Valley firms capitalizing on their technology connections and expertise.

Key Jobs for MBAs

Jobs in investment banks are divided into four areas: corporate finance, sales, trading, and research. Movement between areas isn't unheard of, but since doing your time and moving up the ranks in one area is the quickest way to make a lot of money, most people stay put.

Corporate Finance

Think of corporate finance as financial consulting to businesses. Specific activities range from underwriting the sale of equity or debt for a corporate client to providing advice on mergers and acquisitions, foreign exchange, economic and market trends, and specific financial strategies. When most people refer to investment banking, this is what they mean.

CorpFin (as it is known internally) analysts work 80-hour weeks to help prepare (i.e., proofread and Xerox) pitch books to compete against other banks for prospective clients. They run endless financial models and help prepare (again, proofread and Xerox) due diligence on target companies. After 2 or 3 years, they're bustled off to B-school.

MBAs are brought in at the associate level, where they help underwrite equity (stocks) and fixed-income (bond) offerings, write sections of pitch books, and sit in on client meetings—mostly taking notes—and help devise financial strategies. They also supervise teams of analysts. After 3 or 4 years, they move up to vice president; after another 3 to 5 years, they make it to managing director.

Salary range: $100,000 to $170,000, including bonuses, for associates; $200,000 to $300,000 or more, including bonuses, for VPs.

Sales

Some firms only hire MBAs for sales jobs. Other firms don't even ask about your education. In either case, the bottom line is how well you can sell the new debt and equity issues CorpFin unloads on your desk—and how quickly you can translate news events or a market shift into transactions for your clients. These jobs are usually much less hierarchical than the banking side. Your sales volume and asset growth are what matter.

Salary range: About $40,000, with a $50,000-plus signing bonus for undergrads; MBAs start at $65,000 to $85,000, with a signing bonus. Year-end bonuses fluctuate; if it's been a good year in the market, they can be as high as 80 to 100 percent of base pay.

Trading

When Hollywood directors want to portray the rough, unruly underside of Wall Street, they wheel the cameras onto a trading floor. This is as close to the money as you can get. Trading also commands respect because it's tougher, riskier, and more intense than any other job in finance. Traders manage the firm's risk and make markets by setting the prices—based on supply and demand—for the securities CorpFin has underwritten. Like sales, but more so, you're tied to your desk and phones while the markets are open—but you get to leave after the closing bell.

Beginners fetch endless take-out food and run other thankless errands; more seasoned traders scream and yell when their markets heat up and do the crossword puzzle the rest of the time. Not for the genteel or the faint of heart. A few traders even grow up to be CEOs. Why? Because they know more about the markets and money than anyone else in banking.

Salary range: Similar to that in sales.

Research Analyst

Research departments are generally divided into fixed income (debt) and equity. Both do quantitative research (corporate financing strategies, product development, and pricing models), economic research (forecasts for U.S. and international markets, interest rates, currencies), and individual company coverage. An equity analyst usually focuses on a particular sector—software, oil and gas, or health care, for example.

You move up in this profession by consistently predicting the movement of specific company stocks. The best analysts are ranked annually by *Institutional*

Investor magazine. Their buy, sell, and hold recommendations wield enormous clout, and competition among firms for the top analysts can be intense.

Salary range: For the few undergrads and MBAs hired, starting salaries and signing bonuses are often slightly higher than the rest of investment banking. Senior analysts earn six figures and up (way up).

Job Prospects

Things have been tough on Wall Street over the past few years. The demise of the dot coms ended one major source of revenues for I-banks: IPOs, which are all but impossible to bring to market these days. In 1999, there were 480 initial public offerings, which raised a total of $91.7 billion. In contrast, 2003 saw only 81 IPOs, worth a total of $13.5 billion. The extended market decline has hurt the profits of I-banks' brokerage operations, as investors (and the commissions they pay each time they trade) drop out of the market.

One result of all this turmoil on the Street has been layoffs: According to some, Wall Street employment levels are some 25 percent lower today than they were at their peak in 2000. Still, firms are always looking for new (read: cheaper) bodies; even though they might not be hiring to the extent they did back in the 1990s, banks are still bringing on best-and-brightest hires for analyst and associate programs. But competition for open spots is especially stiff. As a result, getting your foot in the door by doing an internship with a bank should be your top priority if you want to start a career in investment banking.

📂 Key Investment Banks by 2003 Revenue

Company	Revenue ($M)	1-Yr. Change (%)	Employees
Deutsche Bank	54,064	−6.6	62,682
J.P. Morgan Chase & Co.	44,363	2.3	110,453
Morgan Stanley	34,933	7.8	51,196
Merrill Lynch & Co.	27,745	−1.8	48,100
Goldman Sachs Group	23,623	−3.4	19,476
Citigroup Global Markets Holdings	20,722	−2.5	39,000
Lehman Brothers Holdings	17,287	3.0	16,200
Credit Suisse First Boston	11,718	−9.8	18,341
Bear Stearns Companies	7,395	7.3	10,532
Nomura Holdings	7,122	−48.2	14,385
Daiwa Securities Group	3,235	−12.1	11,559
A.G. Edwards	2,499	13.6	15,900
Raymond James Financial	1,498	−1.2	6,000

Sources: Hoover's; WetFeet analysis.

Additional Resources

Institutional Investor Online (www.institutionalinvestor.com)

Investors' Business Daily (www.investors.com)

Knowledge @ Wharton: Finance and Investment
(knowledge.wharton.upenn.edu/category.cfm?catid=1)

McKinsey Quarterly: Financial Services
(www.mckinseyquarterly.com/category_editor.asp?L2=10)

McKinsey Quarterly: Corporate Finance
(www.mckinseyquarterly.com/category_editor.asp?L2=5)

Ohio State University List of Finance Sites
(www.cob.ohio-state.edu/fin/journal/jofsites.htm)

Mutual Funds and Brokerage

Industry Overview

When a large amount of money is needed for any enterprise, from building a factory to funding a corporation to drilling wells in a new oil field, that money is raised from investors—usually a large number of them. Commonly, the enterprise raises that money by either selling ownership shares in itself or simply borrowing it. When ownership is sold, the investor gets shares of stock. When money is borrowed, the investor gets bonds. Stocks and bonds are both securities. Investors buy and sell individual securities through brokers, also called securities dealers.

Additionally, mutual fund companies—and other so-called asset management firms—form funds, which consist of a variety of securities. The asset management company buys and sells the securities in a fund, seeking to maximize its value, and it sells shares in these funds to investors directly and through securities brokers. The mutual fund company charges a fee for picking the securities in a fund. In turn, the shareholder is shielded from the risk of investing in individual securities.

But why lump together two previously distinct areas of the financial services industry—securities brokerage and asset management? Principally because the way your parents invested is not how most people do it these days. More people invest in securities today than ever before, and they have more choices. Not only are there more investments to choose from, including stocks, bonds, real-estate trusts, limited partnerships, and an ever-growing diversity of mutual funds; there are also more ways to invest: full-service brokerages, discount brokerages, and electronic trading for most of us; exclusive opportunities such as hedge funds and venture capital funds for so-called high-net-worth individuals, such as multimillionaires, and institutional investors, such as pension funds, insurance companies, and university endowments.

There is an unimaginably large amount of money chasing investments these days, which is part of the reason that the stock market rose so steeply during the 1990s. Brokerages and mutual funds are the two primary means by which all these investments are made.

Trends

Breaking Glass-Steagall

Companies were chomping at the bit when the Gramm-Leach-Bliley (GLB) Act passed in 1999, essentially dismantling the iron curtain that stood between investment banks and commercial banks since the 1930s. In anticipation, Citibank and Travelers Group merged in 1998, giving what is now called Citigroup a range of services that included investment banking (Salomon Brothers) and a brokerage (Smith Barney) to augment its commercial banking business. Following suit, commercial Chase merged with investment banker J.P. Morgan to form J.P. Morgan Chase, banker UBS with broker Paine Weber, broker Charles Schwab with banker US Trust, all in 2000. Companies are hoping consumers going into bank branches will be enticed by one-stop shopping: "You want a mutual fund with that mortgage refinancing?" Though the mega-merger trend ebbed during the early part of the decade, 2004 saw a rekindling of the acquisitive spirit with Bank of America's takeover of Fleet Financial Services.

Commissions to Fees

The retail brokerage industry is weaning itself from its traditional reliance on trade-based commissions by offering more and more fee-based services, which provide a more regular revenue stream in a volatile market. The fee structure also helps insulate firms from appearances of conflicts of interest as the fee is usually a percentage of assets under management, which means that it's in everyone's interest to see those assets grow. To give you a measure of this trend, fees represented approximately than 25 percent of revenues in 2003, compared to less than 10 percent at the beginning of the decade; fees are expected to account for more than 40 percent of revenues in 5 years.

Scandal du Jour: Timing Is Everything

The financial services industry has had a Comstock Lode of scandals in recent years. Once upon a time one spoke with some incredulity of the transgressions of financial professionals, say, of scandals in which sell-side analysts were accused of delivering fluffed equity reports to curry favor with investment banking clients or to get their kids into the right preschool. Today, the scandals have become accepted as the way America does business. Wrongdoings pervade the industry, from the Armani-pinstripe power broker to the pleated Dockers–wearing mutual fund manager. Early 2004 saw the mutual fund industry fall as firms such as Strong Funds, Canary Capital Partners, Pilgrim Baxter, and Janus Funds were accused of short-selling their own funds or allowing preferred customers to trade fund shares after hours. Even squeaky-clean Charles Schwab, which capitalized on analyst scandals with a scathing ad campaign in 2002, admitted that some of its subsidiaries had engaged in unsavory practices.

Dude, where's my brokerage?

During the trading frenzy of the late '90s, virtual brokers such as E-Trade and Ameritrade were the vehicles of choice for the savvy day trader, but with many of those folks now eating Ramen noodles, these companies have experienced serious declines in activity. Investors increasingly appear to be seeking experienced advice and are willing to pay reasonable incremental costs for help in navigating the current turbulent markets. Though the market rebounded in 2003 and early 2004, retail brokerages have focused on keeping a neat bottom line and resisted aggressive hiring. This is due in no small part to the costs associated with training new brokers—analysts estimate that a full-service brokerage pays about $250,000 to train a new broker and that even seasoned brokers cost firms $150,000 a year.

The strategy most firms have adopted to cope with this fact is by consolidating the industry, Wachovia and Prudential joined forces, creating the third-largest retail brokerage in terms of brokers and customer assets in 2003. In 2002, Ameritrade Holdings purchased Datek Online. Most recently, Bank of America purchased Fleet and its subsidiary Quick & Reilly brokerage. Dozens of regional brokerages are merging as well, in hopes that lashing themselves together will keep them from breaking up in the current economic maelstrom.

How It Breaks Down

Though we divide the industry up into brokerages and mutual funds, within the two segments there are significant differences among the players. You'll want to make sure you not only know which segment you're interested in, but also how the particular company with which you're interviewing is distinguished from the competition.

Brokerage

A broker acts as the intermediary between the buyer and seller in a securities transaction. The buyer and seller, not the brokerage firm, assume the risk. (If the firm acts as the principal or dealer, it deals from its own account and assumes some of the risk itself.) Brokers charge their clients a commission. A full-service firm such as Merrill Lynch charges commissions up to several hundreds of dollars for transactions but offers extras such as tailored research, strategy and planning, and asset management accounts—checking, credit (including lending on margin), and brokerage, all in one convenient package.

A discount broker, such as TD Waterhouse, generally just executes trade orders and issues a confirmation—few or no frills. Frills or no frills, to be authorized to trade on the various exchanges you need to be a registered representative and licensed by the NASD (National Association of Securities Dealers).

Mutual Funds

Whereas brokers act on investors' orders, mutual fund managers raise cash from shareholders and then invest it in stocks, bonds, money-market securities, currencies, options, gold, or whatever else seems likely to make money. Mutual funds often have a specific investment focus—be it income, long-term growth, small cap, large cap, or foreign companies. And managers are restricted in what kinds of investments they can make. Compared to individual portfolios, funds hope to persuade investors they offer several advantages: professional money management; liquidity; and more diversification than most individuals can create or afford in a personal portfolio, particularly now that switching between funds is allowed.

All investors share equally in the gains and losses of a fund, and the most important factor in choosing one—whether to work for or invest in—is probably your tolerance for risk. Bull markets tend to make many funds look good, but a downward turn or a jump in interest rates can have a significant negative impact that may take longer to correct for a fund than in the nimble independent investor's portfolio.

Key Jobs for MBAs

Portfolio Manager Mutual Funds

Portfolio fund managers use their knowledge of investment theory, market experience, research from staff and outside companies, and occasionally plain dumb luck to pick investments for their fund portfolios. Then if the fund outperforms the relevant market indices, the money floods in. If not, the tide pulls the other way. To reach the pinnacle in this profession, count on many years in the ranks of investment advisory and money management. Insiders also point out that passing the SEC's Series 7 exam is necessary in order to be registered and that the Chartered Financial Analyst (CFA) designation is a huge plus for people planning on entering portfolio management.

Salary range: $70,000 to $500,000, with a handful earning more than $1 million.

Wholesaler

Brokers and many of their clients tend to like passive investments, and funds are ideal for these types of people. But they may also want a little more involvement in fund information and more details than Mr. and Mrs. J.Q. Public. Enter the wholesaler from mutual fund XYZ, ready to host a "client appreciation program." Wholesalers market their funds to huge clients such as Merrill and Morgan Stanley, but also must focus on smaller brokers and independent financial advisors. This is nice work if you can get it, and most wholesalers do well.

Salary range: $75,000 to $300,000, with liberal expense accounts for meals and seminars.

Analyst or Researcher

Here you delve into the fundamentals, examining every single feature of a security to determine if it's really a buy. You specialize in a certain industry or an industry segment and come to know the companies that compete there inside out. Expect to give computer screens lots of quality time and to really get cozy with annual reports. If you don't like reading, accounting, crunching numbers, and more reading, you won't be happy here. But it's excellent training for more substantive and lucrative investment-advisory work or portfolio management. Top MBAs sometimes land plum industry assignments; everyone else has to cover trucking and footwear for a while before moving up to telecommunications, technology, and financial services.

Salary range: $50,000 to $100,000, plus bonuses of like amounts or more.

Financial Planner

How is a one-income family going to pay for its kids' college education? How soon, if ever, can a graphic artist retire? Financial planners help people work out these and other difficult money problems. In some ways, this is a thankless job. Even wealthy people don't much enjoy tackling these issues head on, and everyone else actively dreads it. But if you sympathize with that anxiety and know a lot about tax law and different investment strategies, you can do quite well in this business. You can also do it alone with a fair amount of flexibility. Whether you decide to be independent or join a firm, many of these professionals now opt for a CFP (Certified Financial Planner) certification.

Salary range: $60,000 to $120,000. The very best can earn more than $250,000, typically working on a fee or commission basis.

Sales and Marketing

Sales and marketing jobs are similar to product management positions at consumer products companies, but the products are financial products. People in sales no longer focus on fund or investment. They need to be able to sell any one of a growing spectrum of financial products, depending on a customer's short- and long-term needs—and whatever his brother-in-law told him to do last week. This is forecast as one of the strongest areas for jobs in the next 5 to 10 years. Marketers focus on both the long-term picture and specific current product offerings. Who needs what and how much will they pay for it?

Salary range: $40,000 to $100,000, not including bonuses, which can range into six figures.

Job Prospects

With the tremendous proliferation of 401(k), IRA, and other types of retirement plans during the 1990s, more people than ever before can now be classified as investors, either directly or indirectly. The choices for the small-time investor have never been greater, and they include stocks, bonds, mutual funds, real estate trusts, individually managed accounts, and various alternate investments. There's also a range of venue options available should one have an itch to invest, including traditional full-service firms, discount brokerages, and do-it-yourself online trading.

This all boils down to a wide range of career options in a dynamic industry. Though firms say they will hire, in 2004 to 2005 hiring won't be uniformly aggressive. Companies catering to lower-end investors, the discount brokers, are still smarting from their past irrational exuberance. In all, the downward spiral seems to have stopped and some insiders feel that the industry can't continue to grow without doing some substantial hiring. Additionally, the top-tier firms always have slots open for new talent.

Additional Resources

CFA Institute (www.cfainstitute.org)

Financial Analysts Journal (www.aimrpubs.org/faj/home.html)

Institutional Investor Online (www.institutionalinvestor.com)

Investors' Business Daily (www.investors.com)

Knowledge @ Wharton: Finance and Investment (knowledge.wharton.upenn.edu/category.cfm?catid=1)

McKinsey Quarterly: Financial Services (www.mckinseyquarterly.com/category_editor.asp?L2=10)

Ohio State University List of Finance Sites (www.cob.ohio-state.edu/fin/journal/jofsites.htm)

Top Retail Brokerage Companies Ranked by Client Assets, 2003

Firm	Client Assets ($B)	Revenue ($M)	1-Yr. Change (%)	Employees
Merrill Lynch GPC	1,290	8,863	1	48,200
Citigroup PCS (Smith Barney)	1,076	5,827	0	n/a
Wachovia Securities	580	4,200	0	19,000
Morgan Stanley	565	4,017	−1	n/a
UBS Securities	511	3,867	7	18,006
Fidelity Personal Investments	420	n/a	n/a	n/a
A.G. Edwards	248	2,500	14	15,931
Edward Jones	241	2,538	12	29,200
Charles Schwab[1]	222	4,087	0	16,300
TD Waterhouse Investor Svcs.	175	n/a	n/a	5,195
Raymond James & Assoc.[2]	100	1,497	25	6,000
E-Trade Securities[3]	75	886	2	3,500
Ameritrade	70	731	−9	1,732
American Express Investment Svcs.	46	n/a	n/a	n/a
U.S. Bancorp Piper Jaffray	43	701	−5	2,992
Quick & Reilly/Fleet Secs[2]	40	n/a	n/a	n/a

[1]Does not include Schwab Institutional revenue. [2]Prior to takeover by Bank of America.
[3]Does not include Capital Markets revenue:
Source: WetFeet analysis.

Nonprofit and Government

Industry Overview

Nonprofit

Nonprofit organizations are businesses designed to make change, and not in the monetary sense. Granted 501(c)3, or tax-exempt, status by the government, these organizations focus on a wide variety of causes, including everything from the Africa Fund, which promotes human rights, education, and people-to-people exchanges with African countries, to the National Breast Cancer Foundation. Many nonprofit interest groups, such as the Clean Water Fund and the Center on Budget and Policy Priorities, are located in Washington, D.C., where they lobby government on behalf of their causes. Others have offices near state legislatures, where they lobby for the passage of legislation favorable to their causes.

Nonprofits derive their operating revenues from foundations, government grants, membership dues, and fees for services they provide. Nonprofits typically attract people who are passionate about solving social problems; the big upside of working in this sector is that you can make a positive impact on behalf of your organization's cause. The downside is that most jobs in the nonprofit sector, like many in the government sector, don't pay very well.

Government

Some 20 million people work for government—agencies and departments that on a federal, state, or local level handle issues as diverse as highway construction and the protection of wilderness areas, public health programs, subsidies to tobacco farmers, the space program, and fireworks displays on the Fourth of

July. Governments collect taxes and use them to fund programs. That includes everything from a small-town government filling potholes on Main Street, to a big city providing police and fire fighting services, to a state issuing drivers licenses, to the federal government sending troops into combat or making Medicare payments to a long-term health care facility for the elderly.

Federal and state legislators make laws, and city and county supervisors pass ordinances. Executive agencies—from the White House to the state house to city hall—issue regulations. Governments employ armies of civil servants, bureaucrats, lawyers, and specialists of all kinds to implement their policies and staff their programs. These include people who analyze policy and draft legislation for U.S. Senators, people who issue building permits at town hall, and everyone in between.

Even though most employees in this sector enjoy excellent benefits, there can be downsides to working in government. For one thing, the pay is often lower in these positions than in their private-sector equivalents. And in many government positions, jobs are politicized: Your priorities can change with the election cycle, and the program you're working on or the representative you work for may not even be around next year.

Trends

Measuring the Metrics

In an effort to increase their efficiency and effectiveness, governments and nonprofits are increasingly adopting management techniques from business. For example, they're increasingly relying on metrics—quantitative measurements—to gauge their success in achieving goals. This means that government and nonprofit programs, and the staffers who drive them, are increasingly being evaluated by their ability to meet the metrical goals set for them by management (in tandem with funders, in the case of nonprofits). This can be a good thing or a bad thing, depending on whether the right metrics are being used to measure success. It's a lot easier to measure a business's success—just look at the bottom line—and how individuals in that business are contributing to that bottom line than it is to measure nonprofit or government success, where the goal is not to make a profit but to achieve a mission that is difficult to quantify.

Government Outsourcing

In recent years, "reinventing government" has been a catchphrase among policymakers. On the ground, this means that governments are increasingly outsourcing functions and services that were traditionally handled by government agencies to the private sector. For example, municipal governments traditionally provided garbage-removal services in many cities; these days, however, private trash companies often provide these services. The thinking is that the profit motive drives private enterprises to be more efficient than government entities, thus driving down the total cost of outsourced services to society. The reality is less clear, however. The cost of services to society can remain the same (or even increase) even when private enterprises are more efficient than the government service providers they replace, since private enterprises need to charge more for their services than they actually cost to make a profit.

How It Breaks Down

Nonprofits

There are a number of ways to break down the nonprofit sector. For instance, nonprofits can be divided into those that focus on lobbying government on behalf of a cause (interest groups, such as the National Rifle Association) and those that focus on providing services to society (e.g., museums or homes for pregnant teens). But the best way to break down this sector is probably by cause.

To get a sense of the variety of nonprofits, here's a short list of causes and the organizations that serve them:

- Arts and education: Friends of the Library, the Washington Ballet, the New York Philharmonic, the Boy Scouts, the Girl Scouts, 4H, the National Center on Family Literacy

- Civil and human rights: Amnesty International, the American Civil Liberties Union, the National Immigration Forum, the NAACP, Planned Parenthood

- The environment: the Environmental Defense Fund, the National Wildlife Federation, the Nature Conservancy, the Sierra Club

- Economic and social justice: the American Association of Retired Persons, the Center for the Child Care Workforce, the National Low Income Housing Coalition, the Salvation Army, the United Way

Alongside the large national and international nonprofits are myriad local, smaller nonprofits; like their bigger cousins, these break down by mission and include everything from community theater troupes to women's shelters to convalescent homes.

Capitol Hill and Federal Government

The executive branch agencies comprise the largest group of federal government jobs, including the Social Security Administration, the Environmental Protection Agency, the FBI, the National Endowment for the Humanities, the Bureau of Indian Affairs, and the Bureau of Engraving and Printing. (There are also jobs available in agencies under the aegis of the judicial and legislative branches, such as in the Library of Congress or the Congressional Budget Office.) There are two basic types of positions in the various government agencies: civil service positions and political appointments (also called *Schedule C appointments*).

Not all people with federal agency jobs are based in Washington, D.C. Think of all those postal employees out on the streets of America, braving rain, sleet, and snow. Or the diplomat at the U.S. embassy in Cairo. Or the park ranger in

Yellowstone National Park. Think of the bureaucrats in federal office buildings in every major U.S. city, the Bureau of Indian Affairs agent on some isolated reservation in New Mexico, the civilian technician maintaining communications gear in the tropical heat of Guam, the medical researcher culturing bacteria at the Centers for Disease Control in Atlanta.

Congressional jobs, on the other hand, are more concentrated geographically. Congress—the legislative branch—is divided into the House, which consists of one representative from each of 435 districts in the country (and several nonvoting delegates), and the Senate, which is made up of 100 senators, two from each state. Most people who work for the legislative branch of the federal government are based in Washington, D.C. They are on the staffs of legislators or legislative agencies, such as the Library of Congress or the Congressional Budget Office. Congresspeople and senators also maintain staffs in their home districts and states. Every senator and representative hires a staff to assist with his or her job, and this is where many opportunities exist in Washington for young people, provided they have good educations and, usually, good connections.

Like the federal government, state governments consist of various executive-branch agencies along with a legislative body, all of which offer opportunities to job seekers. Similarly, local governments, including those of townships, counties, and cities, offer a range of political and agency job opportunities; consider public health, community development, and court administration.

Nongovernment Political Jobs

In addition to the job opportunities that exist within government, there are plenty of political opportunities that technically are not within government. For example, many people work at lobbying firms (e.g., Patton, Boggs & Blow; Akin, Gump, Strauss, Hauer & Feld; and Verner, Liipfert, Bernhard, McPherson & Hand), nonprofit interest groups (e.g., the American Medical Association or the

Teamsters Union), and think tanks (e.g., the Brookings Institute, the Heritage Foundation, and the Cato Institute). Most of these organizations are located in Washington, D.C., and in the various state capitals. Both the Democratic and the Republican parties have national committees as well as state and local offices where job seekers interested in working for a political party may find opportunities.

Key Jobs for MBAs

Program Director

In larger nonprofits and a handful of small ones, a tier of midlevel management is needed. Duties include oversight and management of a specific program, often including hiring personnel, fund-raising, public relations, and all other administrative and management duties specific to the program area. The program director usually reports directly to the executive director.

Salary range: $40,000 to $60,000.

Executive Director

The grand pooh-bah of the nonprofit organization, the executive director is the equivalent of a CEO and reports directly to the board of directors. He or she is financially accountable for the organization and oversees all strategic planning and management. Depending on the size of the nonprofit, the executive director may be involved with other duties as well, including fund-raising and development, board development, hiring, media relations, program development, and just about anything else that needs to be done.

Salary range: $75,000 and up.

Project Manager

Government project managers work in regulatory agencies, where they manage the process of regulatory review through all its stages. (Think of IRS agents auditing a business or SEC officials investigating charges against a brokerage house.) The job typically requires experience in the regulated industry, an MBA, or equivalent skills.

Salary range: $48,000 to $75,000.

Job Prospects

It can be hard getting a job in either the nonprofit or government sectors. The hiring process is often lengthy, and the competition is fierce. For example, one foundation executive director in California recently received 400 applications for a program manager position. Persistence pays off, though. If you're committed to a particular issue, don't hide it. Volunteering and interning are two very good ways to get in the door at a nonprofit. If you want a government internship, however, you'll most likely have to be a student. That said, a number of government agencies are increasing their hiring numbers, especially in the areas of security and foreign affairs, whereas nonprofits for the most part aren't. So you may find it less of an uphill battle in landing a paying government job versus a nonpaying internship in the nonprofit industry.

Most government agencies have dedicated recruiters who attend college career fairs, industry conferences, and other job placement events. Recruiters tend to be regionally located and look for candidates who have the particular set of skills their area needs. One intelligence agency recruiter says that while many people like giving a resume to someone face to face, resumes submitted online or by mail go through the same process as those given to recruiters directly. So try your luck on agency websites. Government agencies will have recruiting "blitzes" too. Security agencies are recruiting year-round right now, while other agencies such as the GAO accept applications only at certain times of the year. Also, because a huge number of government employees will be retiring in the next 10 to 15 years, there's a lot of advancement potential.

Key Nonprofits by 2003 Revenue

Organization	Revenue ($M)	Total Expenses ($M)	Surplus/ Loss ($M)
Lutheran Industries in America	8,203	6,960	1,243
Mayo Foundation	4,470	4,682	−212
YMCA of the USA National Council	4,271	4,164	107
American National Red Cross	3,952	3,584	411
Catholic Charities USA	2,693	2,584	109
Cleveland Clinic Foundation	2,608	2,622	−14
Salvation Army	2,497	2,492	−5
Goodwill Industries International	2,055	1,982	73
New York Presbyterian Hospital	2,030	1,967	63
Montefiore Medical Center	1,204	1,193	11
Memorial Sloan-Kettering Cancer Center	1,132	1,180	−47
Boys & Girls Clubs of America	1,079	1,002	78
Cedars-Sinai Medical Center	981	920	62
Nature Conservancy	894	1,033	−112
American Cancer Society	774	856	−82
Planned Parenthood Federation of America	767	730	36
Habitat for Humanity	748	621	127
Children's Hospital Medical Center	708	692	17
Boy Scouts of America National Council	665	700	−36
Girl Scouts of the USA	662	675	−13

Source: *Forbes.*

Key U.S. Government Agencies by Number of Civilian Employees, 2003		
Agency/Department	**Federal Budget Outlay (est. $B)**	**Civilian Employees**
U.S. Postal Service	n/a	811,643
Defense	358.0	670,166
Veterans' Affairs	56.9	222,138
Treasury	368.8	147,159
Justice	22.2	131,378
Agriculture	72.8	112,278
Transportation	52.3	102,826
Interior	10.4	72,929
Transportation	54.8	65,542
Health & Human Services	502.0	64,617
Social Security Administration	465.4	65,351

Sources: 2003 U.S. Statistical Abstract (U.S. Census Bureau); WetFeet analysis.

Additional Resources

Careers in Government (www.careersingovernment.com)

McKinsey Quarterly: Nonprofit
(www.mckinseyquarterly.com/category_editor.asp?L2=33)

Nonprofit Career Network (www.nonprofitcareer.com)

The Chronicle of Philanthropy (philanthropy.com)

The Foundation Center (fdncenter.org)

The NonProfit Times (www.nptimes.com)

The U.S. Government Manual (www.access.gpo.gov/nara/browse-gm-01.html)

Real Estate

Industry Overview

The real estate industry's pared-down definition is land. However, it's much more complicated than that. The industry involves the buying, selling, renting, leasing, and management of commercial, residential, agricultural, and other kinds of property, including all the functions that support such activity, such as appraising and financing. The successful realtor is necessarily a shrewd salesperson with a deep knowledge of real estate markets and a broad understanding of the contracts, laws, and tax regulations that apply to real estate transactions.

Thinking big is part of the real estate industry, and grandiose speculation has created some of America's greatest fortunes. John Jacob Astor traded in his empire of beaver pelts for a gamble on uptown Manhattan real estate and in the process became the richest man in America. More recently, moguls like Sam "the grave dancer" Zell and the perennially overreaching Donald Trump have made fantastic fortunes on real estate gambles. Even for nonbillionaires in the industry, the thrill of deal making, the potential for financial reward, and the sociability make real estate a rewarding profession.

Trends

Everyman a Donald Trump

REITs took real estate financing from back rooms and private investors to public markets. As the industry continues to grow into this model, real estate investments are becoming a more common addition to income-earning investment portfolios, both in the public sector as REITS and as private equity for high-net-worth individuals. As stocks and other non–real estate equities have performed poorly, investors have poured even more money into real estate. With this newfound popularity, REITS and the real estate asset class are the big man on the investment campus; and with this trend, increasingly more real estate finance should take place through public markets and investment houses. Of course, some analysts worry that a stock market recovery will spur an outflow of funds from real estate investments.

Finding a Niche

Although the real estate industry has always been attuned to location (say it with us: location, location, location), it hasn't cared what the people in a location want. Companies are now taking more care to market to socioeconomic groups and anticipate the needs of different markets. The industry trend has manifested itself in the form of firms that cater exclusively to particular groups and through the trend of homebuilders in developing "mass customized" homes with luxury options like kitchen islands or high-end appliances available much in the same way car manufacturers offer rich Corinthian leather interiors and air conditioning for a premium.

It's a Little Easier Being Green

Though the real estate industry is hardly considered a tree hugger, there is a major trend toward environmentally sensitive projects. To an extent, wealthy consumers also tend to be eco-conscious ones, pushing homebuilders and developers in an ecologically sensitive direction. Moreover, local, state, and federal legislation has necessitated such construction. Many new developments are "brown fields" projects, which take former industrial sites and make them into residential or office space. The significance of the trend is where these projects are happening; rather than in hippy communes, today's sustainable development is taking place in the heart of corporate America. The Conde Nast building in Times Square in New York City has solar panels affixed to its roof. And architect William McDonough has built a practice around environmentally sensitive buildings, what he has termed "cradle to cradle" design. His work includes the revitalization of the Ford Motor Company's historic River Rouge complex, whose roof is completely covered in sod.

How It Breaks Down

Job opportunities in the industry are divided into four distinct fields: sales, management, development, and acquisition and analysis. Although crossover among these sectors is possible, most people start out specializing in a specific area.

Sales and Leasing

This segment includes everything from residential real estate brokers such as Century 21 and Coldwell Banker to larger corporations that broker bigger commercial properties such as office towers. Grubb & Ellis has one of the largest global brokerage divisions, offering sales and leasing services in many U.S. markets and in Europe. Cushman & Wakefield is another giant, with offices nationwide. Its clients are primarily corporations and other institutions, for which it negotiates sales and leases.

Management

Property managers are responsible for maintaining property values. They deal with tenants, manage finances, and physically tend to the property. Of all the segments of the industry, this one has been hit hardest by the wave of mergers and acquisitions sweeping the industry. Some industry insiders are predicting that 75 percent of the property management firms in operation in 1990 will be out of business by the year 2007. For job seekers, this means fewer jobs as companies look to become more efficient and cut redundant staff.

Development

Developers are responsible for taking a property idea and making it a reality. This is a complex process involving architects, engineers, zoning officials, builders, lenders, and prospective tenants. Development is not always the gravy train some make it out to be. In the early 1990s, when real estate prices crashed, construction dried up and a lot of commercial office space was left vacant. Deprived of rents, a lot of developers had to scramble for survival. Many ventured into other areas of real estate. Today, many of the largest real estate developers are also property owners and managers.

Acquisition and Analysis

Any kind of investing in real estate requires a thorough understanding of how to analyze the value of a property and navigate the maze of land-use regulations, zoning laws, environmental impact reports, financing realities, and other barriers to buying and developing a property. The people who develop, market, and manage REITs and other real estate investments are financial types, often MBAs, who are charged with evaluating and arranging for the purchase of properties.

Key Jobs for MBAs

The great thing about real estate is it's not going away. It's the level of demand and how many jobs the market can support that will fluctuate. For salespeople, there's plenty of competition. On the management side, there is the popularity of rental housing and a rising number of job opportunities in apartment and assisted-living management. Those who want security can find work as appraisers, as these jobs are less affected by the industry cycle.

Consultant or Advisor

With the increase in institutional investing, demand for this type of expert has risen. Prior experience in investing or management is necessary. A real estate advisor is generally good with statistics and excels at dealing with clients.

Salary range: $50,000 and up.

Developer

A developer makes property plans come to life. To become a developer, you'll need excellent communication skills and a strong understanding of all aspects of the real estate industry. Most developers start out in entry-level positions with a developer or contractor and then work their way up.

Salary range: $50,000 to $100,000 or more.

Entrepreneur

A real estate entrepreneur buys property for the purpose of making money. Success as an entrepreneur takes an equal mix of industry smarts and good fortune. Just remember that although many people have made fortunes in real estate, even more haven't.

Salary range: The sky's the limit, but the threat of bankruptcy is very real.

Job Prospects

Unlike much of the rest of the economy, the real estate industry has been doing quite well, with many leading firms chalking up double-digit top-line growth in 2003. Though the robustness varies between sectors, with the residential side of real estate doing best, the industry is hardly in the hangdog state that nearly every other part of the economy seems to be in.

Nevertheless, without solid connections in the industry, you may have a hard time establishing yourself. Real estate veterans rely on the advice of contacts to help make recruiting decisions. Rather than using traditional recruiting processes, firms often bring on new talent through personal networks and word of mouth. It's even harder to break into the elite club of real estate investment finance.

If you don't aspire to join the elite ranks of real estate investment management, you still have before you a wealth of rewarding positions in property management, real estate services, and residential brokerages, as well as very challenging development roles in corporate real estate. Beware though: Skills in one real estate market aren't necessarily transferable to other markets. Select your location carefully. And once you're in, be prepared to ride the roller coaster of a cyclical industry. Although the real estate industry is in a protracted boom period right now, veterans assure us that busts will come, and those busts won't be pretty.

Additional Resources

Knowledge @ Wharton: Real Estate
(knowledge.wharton.upenn.edu/category.cfm?catid=8)

Institute of Real Estate Management (www.irem.org)

Realtor.org (www.realtor.org)

Key Real Estate Companies by 2003 Revenue			
Company	**Revenue ($M)**	**1-Yr. Change (%)**	**Employees**
Cendant Corp.	18,192	29	87,000
Centex Corp.*	10,363	14	16,532
Pulte Homes	9,049	21	10,800
Lennar Corp.	8,908	22	10,572
D.R. Horton	8,728	30	6,348
The Trump Org.	8,500	0	15,000
KB Home	5,775	17	5,100
NRT**	4,039	28	52,801
The Ryland Group	3,444	20	2,558
Host Marriott Corp.	3,442	−7	182
Equity Office Properties Trust	3,397	−6	2,400
Hovnanian Enterprises	3,202	26	3,249
The LeFrak Org.**	2,800	−26	16,200
Simon Property Group	2,408	−1	4,040
Westfield Group	2,092	57	n/a
Tishman Realty & Construction**	1,980	21	900
Equity Residential	1,834	−8	6,000
Lincoln Property Co.**	1,766	31	5,000
CB Richard Ellis Group	1,630	39	13,500
Vornado Realty Trust	1,614	5	2,700

*2004 figures. **2002 figures.
Sources: Hoover's; WetFeet analysis.

Industries

Telecommunications

Industry Overview

Telecommunications has made it possible to speak or exchange text and/or images
with virtually anyone in the world by pushing a few buttons. This immediacy of
communication has had dramatic effects: Worldwide commerce is easier; totalitarian
regimes are more vulnerable to dissenting voices carried by fax or e-mail; shopping
is more convenient. High-tech telecommunications in particular, including fax,
e-mail, and wireless phones, let families and friends stay in contact more easily
and less expensively. As reference material moves online, the Web makes academic
and business research possible with less need to go to a physical library.

Telecommunications is a mammoth industry, comprising companies that make
hardware, produce software, and provide services. Hardware includes a vast
range of products that enable communication across the entire planet, from
video broadcasting satellites to telephone handsets to fiber-optic transmission
cables. Services include running the switches that control the phone system,
making access to the Internet available, and configuring private networks by
which international corporations conduct business. Software makes it all work,
from sending and receiving e-mail to relaying satellite data to controlling
telephone switching equipment.

The breakup of AT&T in 1984 created the modern telecommunications industry,
subjecting phone companies to free-market forces for the first time. The long-
distance market became competitive almost immediately, but the so-called Baby
Bells fought a rear-guard action against letting companies like AT&T or MCI enter
the local phone market. But the Telecommunications Act of 1996 deregulated

local phone markets. Proponents say deregulation makes telecommunications services more competitive, benefiting consumers. Critics say it gives a few, giant companies untrammeled sway over our ability to communicate with each other.

Trends

A New Meaning for "Convergence"

Even the big long-distance carriers want to get into the local phone-service ring—and because of deregulation, they're starting to do just that. The reason is that local service has higher margins than long distance. Meanwhile, the Baby Bells are trying to build their residential long-distance businesses; indeed, Verizon now offers long distance in six states, and SBC does the same in five states). The Baby Bells are also trying to horn in on the lucrative business long-distance market. The result? Greater competition in almost every sector of telecom—and lower prices, to boot.

Turnaround

The telecom industry was extremely stung by the economic downturn of recent years. However, there are at least a few signs that the industry may be starting to stage a recovery. Industry expenditures and revenues are both expected to rise in 2004, the first rise in both areas since 2000. The biggest revenue gains are supposed to come in the wireless services sector. At the same time, companies seem to be hiring again—especially startups and companies emerging from Chapter 11, as well as companies in areas like wireless communications and computing, and Internet telephony.

VoIP

Voice over Internet Protocol makes it possible to send phone calls as "data packets" across networks—no longer must phone calls travel through local phone company wirelines. Local telephone companies, long-distance companies, and cable companies are all fighting for their piece of this potentially large new market. Indeed, long-distance providers Sprint and MCI are both working with cable provider Time Warner to bring VoIP service to cable subscribers, and AT&T, Verizon, SBC, and Qwest are all working to bring their own VoIP offerings to market.

How It Breaks Down

Before the Telecommunications Act of 1996, a variety of regulations divided telecommunications artificially—cable TV companies were prohibited from offering local telephone service, video programming over phone lines was banned, and local service companies and long-distance service providers were forbidden from competing in each other's markets. The Telecommunications Act lifted these competitive restrictions. One regulatory barrier that remains prohibits service providers from manufacturing telecommunications equipment. The cleanest way to break this industry down, then, is between those who make the software and hardware and those who provide various services.

Service Providers

These companies provide local and long-distance wireline telephone service. Industry insiders call this *POTS*, for plain old telephone service. Wireline providers include the large long-distance service providers—AT&T, MCI, and Sprint—and the RBOCs (the Baby Bells) such as SBC Communications and BellSouth. A new generation of companies is laying fiber-optic wire networks to handle the rapidly increasing data traffic, including Qwest and Level 3.

Wireless Service Providers

Marked by carrier consolidation and partnering to augment geographic reach and gain economies of scale, wireless communication services have shaken up the telecom service industry. They have also brought telecommunications to the far corners of the earth, including parts of Africa and South America where there's no existing wireline infrastructure, and have made local markets far more competitive in the United States.

Satellite Telecommunication Services

Satellite telecom services breaks down into fixed satellite services such as INTELSAT; low earth orbit companies (LEOs), which include Iridium and mega-LEO Teledesic (controlled by Craig McCaw); direct broadcast satellite companies such as DIRECTV; and the global positioning system (GPS). Satellite services include everything from navigation systems (such as you can expect to find in the dash of your automobile sometime in the near future) to video broadcast and data transmission.

Internet Service Providers

ISPs consist of those companies that make it possible for you to go online—Microsoft, AOL, MindSpring, and the RBOCs. The Internet, which has become an integral part of the telecommunications industry, is also the vehicle by which a huge dose of talent and energy has been added to telecom as voice and data networks converge.

Customer Premise Equipment (CPE) Manufacturers

Telecommunication service providers are the biggest customers of telecommunications equipment makers. When they sell a service to a company, for instance, they purchase the switch, which can serve anywhere from 15 to 100,000 people, as well as other CPE—everything from telephones to voice-mail systems to private branch exchanges (PBXs). Local area networks require their own routers, switches, and hubs. The big players here include Lucent Technologies, Nortel, Fujitsu, Siemens, and Alcatel.

Networking Equipment and Fiber Optics Manufacturers

Networking equipment includes the stuff that makes the local area network operative, including routers, hubs, switches, and servers. Fiber optics consists of the optical fiber and fiber-optic cable, transmitters, receivers, and connectors that carry data and voice messages. The biggest switch makers are Nortel and Lucent. Cisco and 3Com are among the biggest makers of networking equipment.

Wireless and Satellite Communication Equipment Manufacturers

These are different categories that we've grouped together. The radio-based communications systems, the switches, transmission, and subscriber equipment for this sector differ from those the wireline service providers use. Large players in wireless equipment include Motorola, Qualcomm, Hughes Electronics, Sony, and NEC. Satellite communication equipment makers include Comcast and Loral Space, as well as a number of cable companies, such as Cox Communications, DIRECTV, EchoStar Communications, and TCI International.

Key Jobs for MBAs

Product Manager

Essentially, product managers make the product happen. Product managers determine what service or product they'll sell to the end user, then help develop it, be it wireless service, DSL, caller ID, or voice mail. On the manufacturing side, they need to know the technology or show some knowledge about it. This position generally requires an MBA or similar experience with another company, preferably in networking or data communications.

Salary range: $60,000 to $125,000.

Public Relations and Government Relations

The role the government has played in regulating telecommunications has resulted in a number of jobs within the major companies to work with the government and press to enhance relations. These include lobbying government officials, helping draft legislation, and working with the press to garner favorable coverage for regulations your company supports.

Salary range: $50,000 to $150,000.

Job Prospects

Telecom companies built staff and infrastructure like crazy during the boom times of the 1990s. In the early 2000s, many telecoms used layoffs, massive reorganization, and spinoffs to offset losses—making the outlook bleak for job seekers. More recently, though, the industry has been recovering somewhat, and the outlook for job seekers is looking more favorable.

In the long term, employment in the industry is expected to grow, but not at breakneck speed. According to the Bureau of Labor Statistics, telecom employment is expected to grow by 12 percent between 2000 and 2010, slower than the 15 percent average growth projected for all industries combined. In this varied field, demand for workers, or lack of it, will be based mostly on technology. For example, as new voice recognition technology improves productivity, jobs like telephone and directory assistance operators will continue to decrease in number. But the need for engineers who develop that technology will increase.

The outlook is good in telecom sectors that are bringing exciting new technologies to market. High-speed data services, voice communications over the Internet, wireless networking: These and other technologies will increase the need for electrical and electronics engineers, computer software engineers, systems analysts, customer service professionals, and the likes.

If you want to work in an industry that requires you to learn fast and adapt quickly, this is it.

Key Telecommunications Companies by 2003 Revenue			
Company	Revenue ($M)	1-Yr. Change (%)	Employees
Siemens	86,467	4	417,000
Verizon Communications	67,752	0	203,100
SBC Communications	40,843	−5	168,000
NEC Corporation	39,788	4	145,807
Fujitsu Limited	38,529	2	157,044
Nokia	37,031	18	51,359
AT&T	34,529	−9	61,600
BT Group	29,596	13	104,700
Motorola	27,058	2	88,000
Sprint	26,197	−2	66,900
BellSouth	22,635	1	76,000
Cellco Partnership	22,489	17	43,900
Cisco Systems	18,878	0	34,000
Comcast Holdings	18,348	47	68,000
AT&T Wireless Services	16,695	7	31,000
Alcatel	15,731	−10	60,486
Cingular Wireless	15,483	5	39,400
Qwest Communications	14,288	−7	47,000
Lucent Technologies	8,470	−31	34,500
Ericsson	2,433	−8	4,460
Sources: Hoover's; WetFeet analysis.			

Additional Resources

CrossNodes (networking.earthweb.com)

McKinsey Quarterly: Telecom
(www.mckinseyquarterly.com/category_editor.asp?L2=22)

Telecommunications Online (www.telecoms-mag.com)

Venture Capital

Industry Overview

Underneath their moneyed mystique, venture capitalists are essentially glorified middlemen, and their modus operandi is easily explained. In a nutshell, a VC firm acts as a broker for institutional or "limited partner" investors such as pension funds, universities, and high-net-worth individuals, all of whom pay annual management fees to have their money invested in high-risk, high-potential-yield start-up companies.

After amassing a certain sum from the limited partner investors—usually between $10 million and $1 billion—the VC firm parcels out the fund to a portfolio of fledgling private companies, each of which hands over an equity stake in its business. In other words, the VC industry is predicated on a simple swap of the VC's financing for an ownership stake in the company's success, often (but by no means always) before the company has begun generating revenue. VC funding has nourished some of corporate America's greatest success stories when they were still baby businesses—FedEx, Intel, Sun Microsystems, and Apple, to name a few.

Since the VC firm has a vested interest in its start-ups' success, partners will generally sit on several boards of directors, offering advice and additional resources to help businesses grow. In the event that one of its start-ups merges with or is bought out by a larger company or goes public, any windfall is divvied up between the company, the VC firm, and the limited partner investors. Typically, the VC firm distributes 70 to 80 percent of the return on its investments to the various limited partners and keeps the rest for itself.

Trends

The Fundraising Bandwagon

In 2003, VC firms raised the smallest amount of money since 1995. But 2004 is another story. Battery Ventures, Charles River Associates, Kleiner Perkins, New Enterprise Associates, and Kodiak Venture Partners are a few of the firms with new funds ready to deploy. New Enterprise even topped one billion, at $1.1 billion, the first billion-dollar fund since 2001. Technology Crossover Ventures came close with its $900 million fund. Generally, however, these funds are smaller than their predecessors. All this new money, along with the stock market's success in 2003 and early 2004, has created rising valuations for early and later-stage venture-backed firms. The 6- to 9-month fundraising process requiring 30 to 40 first visits in 2003 is dramatically down, with many entrepreneurs canceling first-time meetings.

Economic Optimism

Improvements in the economy are partly responsible for the mini-mania gripping the VC industry. Since 2002, the Nasdaq has nearly doubled. The IPO market has come back, with a multi-billion IPO for Google in summer 2004 and a multimillion one for Salesforce.com providing hefty returns for the VCs that backed them. As of June 21, 2004, with 16 IPOs on the docket, June was the biggest month for offerings since October 2000. More M&A deals are getting done, too, with large firms using their increasing capitalizations to buy venture-backed start-ups. And IDC, a research firm, expects worldwide IT spending to rise 5 percent in 2004, to $915 billion, creating serious opportunity after 3 years of flat to negative growth. A stock market crash could put a halt to M&A and spending, and some economic indicators suggest weakness, but in summer 2004 there's overall optimism that the economy is on a rising tide.

Offshore Fever

Many venture investors are encouraging their startups to move jobs overseas, saving labor costs while increasing competitiveness. An informal Forrester Research survey of venture capitalists suggests 20 to 25 percent of the companies they invest in are committed to moving jobs overseas—including some of the industry's biggest names, such as Kleiner Perkins Caufield & Byers, Sevin Rosen Funds, and Norwest Ventures. Says Forrester Vice-President John C. McCarthy, "The venture guys are driving offshore as much as anyone."

How It Breaks Down

There are many kinds of players in the VC world, from traditional VC firms to funds operated by publicly owned corporations. Some are tightly focused—by stage of investment, region, or type of industry—but most have a much broader focus. Here's a rough breakdown of the industry:

Private VC Firms (Early- to Mid-Stage)

Firms in this segment follow the classic VC model: Find an entrepreneur with a great idea and business plan, sprinkle with cash, bake for several years, and sell for a hefty chunk of change. Early-stage (or seed) investments are the riskiest, since many start-ups tank. Still, they often provide the highest returns since investors coming in early can pay a lower price for a given share of equity. In the 1990s, as many traditional VC firms started to focus on middle- and late-stage investments, seed financing increasingly became the province of newer firms and angel investors—entrepreneurs or corporate executives who've made it big and have money to spend.

Private VC Firms (Mid- to Late Stage)

These firms, many of which also operate at the seed level, provide funds to companies that are already established—those that have a product, sufficient employees, and perhaps even revenues. At these stages, firms inject more capital into the company to help it become profitable so that it will attract enough interest to either be acquired by a larger company or go public.

Growth Buyout Funds

Some VCs have moved into growth buyouts of larger private companies or divisions of public companies. These funds invest larger amounts of capital—up to $100 million—in exchange for a significant minority or majority position in the company. By focusing on stable, growing (and often profitable) companies, buyout funds don't have to wait long before they can cash in on the company's IPO or sale. There's less risk—unless market factors cause the delay of an IPO, for example. The funded company and its earlier investors benefit from having a prestigious late-stage investor add credibility on Wall Street come IPO time.

Financial Services Firms

Where there's money, of course you'll find I-bankers. Banks such as Morgan Stanley and Citicorp will invest in the later stages. The aim is pretty much the same as that of the VCs: to make a killing through either an IPO or an acquisition.

Corporate Funds

As opposed to private funds, whose primary goal is monetary gain, corporate funds have the added goal of strategically investing in companies whose business relates in some way to the corporation's own. For example, Microsoft invested in Qwest Communications, a telecom company that is building a fiber-optic network, to help it deliver NT-based software.

Key Jobs for MBAs

Staffing needs and titles vary greatly from one venture capital firm to the next. Many funds consist solely of partners and support staff. Others hire a limited number of undergraduates and MBAs as analysts and associates with the expectation that most will return to get their business degrees or join start-ups within a few years. (Keep in mind that while the terms "analyst" and "associate" usually refer to undergrads and MBAs or experienced hires, respectively, at some firms the titles are reversed.)

General Partner

These are the people with their names on the door. General partners raise the money for the fund and make the final decisions on which companies to invest in. General partners, the professional members of a venture capital firm, are usually required to contribute a small amount of their own money to their fund. They manage the fund's investments and generally take a 20 to 30 percent cut of the carry from the fund. General partners are expected to provide a wealth of business advice and industry contacts to the entrepreneurs they back. They often sit on the boards of many companies and are deeply involved in decisions about exit strategies—that is, when to cash out by taking the company public or selling it.

Salary range: $200,000 to $500,000 and up, plus the potential of millions in profits.

Junior Partner

Junior partners are just that: junior versions of the general partners. Usually, junior partnerships are viewed as training for general partnerships and junior partners perform similar duties albeit on a reduced scale. Also reduced is their personal stake in the fund itself.

Salary range: $150,000 to $300,000, plus a limited amount of carry, or percentage of profits.

VP or Associate

Some firms hire MBAs or people with business experience (usually in leveraged buyouts or investment banking) as vice presidents or associates. Associates screen business plans, make cold calls on prospective investments, and on occasion make on-site visits to portfolio companies. At this level, compensation, while still tied to the overall performance of the fund, can take the form of a flat bonus rather than a percentage of the fund.

Salary range: $75,000 to $250,000, including bonus; VPs earn at the higher end.

Job Prospects

Finding a job in VC isn't hopeless, but it will be hard. "It's hard to target. There isn't a formula you can control. It's more ambiguous than getting a job at Procter & Gamble or in management consulting," says an insider. Firms are selective, and finding a job requires good luck. "The way to gain access to this industry is to do something great that is visible to people in this industry," says an insider. "There's not a lot on your resume that will tell whether you will do well in venture capital." Operating experience at a technology company is a must in today's environment. "Go somewhere where you can build a base of judgment and behavior in business, and excel in some capacity," says an insider. "Be the product manager of the best, newest PDA. It doesn't have to be a small company. Interact with thought leaders, take risks, and succeed where there is something to be gained." Finally, if you're hell-bent on a career in VC, don't give up. "If you strategize, are smart about looking for the opportunities, there will be some amount of opportunity for you to get in there," says an insider.

Rank	Firm	Early-Stage Deals (#)
	Top VC Firms for Entrepreneurs in 2003	
1	Maryland Technology Development Corp.	15
2	Maryland Dept. of Business and Economic Development	12
3	Village Ventures	11
4	Draper Fisher Jurvetson	9
	Mobius Venture Capital	9
	Sevin Rosen Funds	9
7	Band of Angels	8
	Mayfield Fund	8
10	Highland Capital Partners	7
	Ignition Partners	7
	ITU Ventures	7
	Matrix Partners	7
	New Enterprise Associates	7
	U.S. Venture Partners	7
	Source: *Entrepreneur*, July 2004.	

Additional Resources

Harvard Business School Venture Capital & Principal Investment Club (sa.hbs.edu/vc)

National Venture Capital Association (www.nvca.org)

PricewaterhouseCoopers MoneyTree Survey (www.pwcmoneytree.com)

VentureReporter.net (venturereporter.net)

Industries

Careers

Asset Management

Career Overview

If money makes the world go 'round, the Earth would grind to a screeching halt without the asset management industry. Asset management is the business of making money with money—or at least trying to. When we say "money," we're not talking about salaries and bonuses (which can indeed be significant), but the gains you endeavor to make for investors who have forked over their cash in hopes that you, through your market savvy and keen instincts, can turn their nest egg into a fancy omelet with toast and hash browns on the side.

Asset managers manage money—other people's money, and gobs of it. Generally, they convert that money into assets—stocks, bonds, derivatives, and other types of investments—and try to make that money make more money as fast as possible. Mutual funds, for instance, hire asset managers; so do corporations with lots of money sitting around, banks, and high-net-worth individuals.

Asset managers have one simple goal: to invest other people's money wisely and profitably. Asset managers use a combination of investment theory, quantitative tools, market experience, research, and plain dumb luck to pick investments for their portfolios, ranging from high-risk stocks to commercial real estate to cash accounts.

Requirements

As an asset manager, you can't just bet your hunches. The profession requires excellent quantitative and analytical skills—if you hated statistics, you may want to look elsewhere.

But asset management isn't just a matter of adding up the numbers. It requires the organizational skills—and nerve—to make split-second decisions with millions of dollars riding on the line. And though the profession has seen tremendous growth in the last decade, it's still tough to break into, especially for those who only have an undergraduate degree. Sometimes MBAs work as fund managers right out of school, though more often they start as analysts in order to prove they have the right combination of caution and chutzpah to make a great asset manager.

Competition for jobs is fierce at all levels, but if you have strong quantitative and analytical skills, good nerves, and can consistently beat the market, then there's probably a place for you. Networking and a single-minded pursuit of your goal are big helps, too.

Generally, MBAs come aboard as researchers or analysts. Sometimes they're hired as fund managers, but only if they have a track record of success as both managers and investors. Because competition is tough, it's important to know a lot about the company interviewing you, and to show an intimate knowledge of its investment strategies.

Analysts and researchers generally serve at least 2 years before they come up for consideration as fund managers. You are also more likely to get an asset-manager position earlier if you run smaller portfolios for institutional asset managers or private banks that offer services to the wealthy. On the mutual-fund side, you might become co-portfolio manager, sharing the management responsibility with a senior manager. The larger the pool of assets, the fiercer the competition.

There is no single prerequisite to becoming an asset manager. It all comes down to how much money you can make with other people's money. That said, virtually all successful asset managers possess these skills:

Quantitative and Analytical Skills

Asset managers have to be able to read spreadsheets and earnings reports. And they have to be able to take those numbers and crunch them into financial models and future projections. Even if you're dealing with less volatile investments such as bonds or real estate, you have to do the math in order to stay ahead of conventional wisdom. Classes in accounting and statistics are a big help, as are jobs that require number crunching, from I-banking to management consulting.

Managerial and Organizational Skills

Whether you're a researcher or a fund manager, you'll have to keep track of reams of facts in order to glean the really important information. Furthermore, you'll have to be able to make decisions—and execute them—quickly and accurately. Delay can cost big money. Finally, you need to be able to motivate and manage a talented staff of researchers and analysts if you work your way up to portfolio manager. Without their coordinated efforts, you may not have the information you need to make the best decision possible.

Professional Licensing

In general, asset managers who work behind the scenes and make the big decisions don't need professional licensing. But you probably will if you're dealing with the public at all, especially if you're in a position to make buy and sell recommendations directly to a client. For example, you may need an NASD license (Series 7, 63, or 65), or certain insurance licenses. Employers will generally give you the time to get such licenses once you're hired, and may even pay the costs.

Career Tracks

Mutual funds, such as Vanguard or T. Rowe Price, are perhaps the most visible road into asset management. Hedge funds—which specialize in high-risk, high-return investments for wealthy clients—also offer opportunities for would-be asset managers.

Large investment and commercial banks, from J.P. Morgan Chase to Citibank, as well as private firms such as Soros Fund Management, offer private banking—that is, asset management for wealthy clients with very large private accounts. Some large-scale investment institutions such as universities and retirement funds hire their own investment staffs, though often they rely on mutual funds and other investment management companies to make decisions for them, from Fidelity to the Capital Group.

If you prefer real estate to stocks and bonds, you can work for a real estate investment trust (REIT) such as Cornerstone Properties. REITs operate like mutual funds, except they buy and sell hotels and shopping malls rather than stocks and bonds. Finally, there are a number of boutique asset-management firms that take money from a small group of wealthy clients and invest in specialized areas such as start-up companies.

No matter where you work, asset management boils down to this: researching and analyzing potential investments and deciding where exactly to allocate funds. Of course, companies require a raft of other employees, including corporate managers, IT specialists, marketing and sales people, and back-office staff. But if you want to be on the front lines where big investment decisions are made, you will fulfill one of these three functions:

Researcher

The job of the researcher is implied in the name: He or she gathers the primary source material from which investment decisions are made, such as SEC filings and quarterly earning reports. When they start, researchers spend their time learning the philosophy of those running the portfolio. Researchers then work to ensure that the fund manager has the information necessary to make the decisions he or she needs to make with that philosophy in mind.

As time passes, researchers are granted more independence and may even perform the kind of higher-level analyses that lead to actual decisions about buying and selling. Generally, researchers are hired straight out of undergraduate or B-school programs. MBAs, of course, enjoy better odds of getting hired and generally command better salaries. All candidates should have strong quantitative, analytical, and organizational skills.

Analyst

Analysts take the work of researchers and apply higher-level financial modeling to make specific recommendations to portfolio managers about which securities to buy or sell. In addition to crunching numbers, they may conduct more subjective research, such as meeting with representatives of potential investment companies in order to assess management style. Or they may pick the brains of sell-side analysts at brokerages and other financial institutions to gather tips about specific investments and to gauge overall market trends. Seasoned analysts may even participate in developing overall investment strategies for their investment fund.

Fund Manager

Fund managers are the people who decide what, when, and how much to buy or sell. They must work to ensure that their fund's overall investment philosophy is borne out in actual investments, and be willing to change course midstream if their strategy isn't working. They must also make sure their decisions are executed, which means following up on the work of traders and other agents. And of course they're responsible for managing the work of researchers and analysts in order to ensure that the fund manager is receiving the best, most complete information possible.

Besides poring over numbers, they spend a great deal of time meeting with managers of companies they might invest in to make more subjective, managerial assessments. Finally, they may have to engage in a certain amount of marketing and public relations—for example, helping to design sales strategies or talking to the press.

Job Outlook

Anyone considering a career in asset management should be keenly aware that markets not only go up, but also go down—sometimes way down. There was a time, in another century, when the markets were on a rocket ship to the moon. The year was 1999 and the entire financial industry was, well, partying like it was 1999.

The hangover from all that partying made the financial services industry a much more sober place. The rookies were largely sidelined and investments became once again the bailiwick of professionals. The market quietly inched back up in late 2003 and early 2004. Worldwide mutual fund investment shot up 9 percent in the last quarter of 2003 to $13.96 trillion, a 30 percent increase over the third quarter of 2002. Still, the upsurge in the market hasn't translated into commensurate levels of hiring.

The hiring picture doesn't look brighter when you consider the M&A activity taking place in the industry. As more and more firms follow Citigroup's lead by increasing their service offering through the roll-up of second-tier players, you, the job seeker, get hurt by these efficiencies. Bank of America's acquisition of Fleet Financial at the end of 2003 continued this trend. But don't get too discouraged. Asset managers and brokerage firms are still hiring, albeit in a more modest capacity than in the past. There is still money to be made, but you will have to make it the old-fashioned way, by earning it. And you will earn it through hard work and a proven ability to create real financial value for your clients. Amidst the broken chandeliers and shattered vases of the postbubble financial industry, some potentially exceptional opportunities still lurk. So if you do manage to find (and keep) a job in the industry, you can still expect to make a solid living and retain something of a life, particularly compared to the slave-labor existence of your investment banking peers.

Though firms say they will hire in 2004 to 2005, hiring won't be uniformly aggressive. Companies catering to lower-end investors, the discount brokers, are still smarting from their past irrational exuberance. In all, the downward spiral seems to have stopped and some insiders feel that the industry can't continue to grow without doing some substantial hiring. Additionally, the top-tier firms always have slots open for new talent.

Additional Resources

Financial Analysts Journal (www.aimrpubs.org/faj/home.html)

Knowledge @ Wharton: Finance and Investment
(knowledge.wharton.upenn.edu/category.cfm?catid=1)

Investors' Business Daily (www.investors.com)

Institutional Investor Online (www.institutionalinvestor.com)

McKinsey Quarterly: Financial Services
(www.mckinseyquarterly.com/category_editor.asp?L2=10)

Ohio State University List of Finance Sites
(www.cob.ohio-state.edu/fin/journal/jofsites.htm)

Brand Management

Career Overview

A formal definition of brand management is tough to pin down because the actual job description varies widely across the vast universe of consumer products companies. Many consumer products companies have at least one thing in common, though: They're part of huge conglomerates that produce many name-brand products. Size gives them economies of scale, and a diversity of products gives them protection against down cycles. Which is not to say that cute little mail-order pickle-and-jam companies don't crop up every now and then and make a serious go of it. They do. These places aren't where the majority of the jobs are, however—at least not until Unilever or Nestlé takes them over.

Success in consumer products (also known as packaged goods)—which is where most brand management careers are found—is all about marketing, often by promoting a brand name. The competition is ferocious for shelf space, so package design, marketing, and customer satisfaction are key elements. In brand management, you'll be responsible for managing all of these elements as they relate to the brand to which you're assigned.

The basic analogy for brand management is that brands are treated like businesses within the company and brand managers are essentially small-business owners. The job involves

- Monitoring the competitive landscape of the category in which your brand competes.
- Developing strategies to exploit market opportunities.
- Executing those strategies with the help of a cross-functional team.
- Delivering the sales volume, market share, and profit projections for the business.

Brand managers craft elegant business plans and submit them to senior management. Then, when the price of the key ingredient in their product goes through the roof because of locust plagues, they rewrite the business plan from scratch with many more contingencies. They focus on the minutiae of a daily sales volume report, and they dream big dreams when it's time to update the vision for the brand. They approach upper-level management for capital to fund a new product launch or a line extension in much the same way that small business owners go to venture capitalists or banks to fund expansion.

Requirements

Brand management is considered part of the marketing function, and most aspiring brand managers have had some experience in advertising, promotions, or sales. However, consumer packaged goods companies are very interested in candidates who have honed their analytical and leadership skills in other disciplines, including consulting, investment banking, or strategic planning. If you have no previous experience in marketing, a summer internship can be enormously helpful. Many companies offer summer internships that often result in a job offer after graduation.

Recruiters look for leadership, analytical skills, problem solving, teamwork, and creativity. Successful applicants should have at least an undergraduate degree in business, liberal arts, or a related field. Philosophy majors and engineers are equally welcome to apply, if they can demonstrate skills in the five areas just mentioned. Most companies look for candidates with at least a 3.5 GPA. The more work experience and leadership and teamwork experience (in a sorority/fraternity, school club, or sports team) you can show, the better.

Career Tracks

The career track at most companies features plenty of opportunities for cross-functional experience and varied work assignments. At some companies, experience in functions other than marketing has become a prerequisite for advancement. One insider reports that in her 25-year career at Procter & Gamble, she has held seven different jobs in departments ranging from marketing to cost accounting to corporate recruiting.

Despite flexibility in career path development, there are clearly defined entry-level positions, and MBAs enter as assistant brand managers.

The path from assistant brand manager to brand manager is a progression from executing to developing strategy. Continuing along the path involves a shift from participating in cross-functional teams to leading them and from monitoring a business budget to assuming profit and loss responsibility. At some point along this path, most companies send aspiring managers out into the field for extensive sales training, a.k.a. the reality check. The annals of brand management are full of tales of "brilliant" strategy that the sales force could not execute in a store. In general, marketing analysts support multiple small businesses or one big one; assistant brand managers run a small business; and brand managers manage one large business or a portfolio of two or three smaller ones. Marketing directors, a catchall term for the levels beyond brand manager, oversee a major portfolio of brands.

Assistant Brand Manager

As an assistant brand manager, it is your job to coordinate the various marketing functions, including packaging, advertising, promotions, and public relations, in order to execute the marketing plan.

In the course of executing the marketing plan, you will head up a number of cross-functional teams that work on various parts of your business. For example, a product improvement project may bring together R&D, marketing research, packaging, finance, and operations. A change in your consumer promotion plan might require a coordinated effort between representatives from promotions and operations.

Assistant brand managers shift gears all day long. One minute they're brainstorming new promotion ideas, the next they're wading through monthly volume projections.

Brand Manager

Our insiders describe this role as being captain of a ship, guiding your cross-functional crew through such treacherous waters as annual plans, new product launches, competitive analyses, promotional strategies, and capacity planning at your production facilities. The safe port you're steering toward consists of the volume, market share, and profit targets for your brand—you now own the bottom line on the profit-and-loss (P&L) statement for your business.

You also take on additional responsibilities at the business unit, division, or corporate level. These responsibilities might range from serving on a company-wide task force that is reviewing trade spending across different brands to leading the recruiting team at your alma mater. You are also responsible for the performance of the marketing analysts and assistant brand managers who work on your business.

Marketing Director

Marketing directors are responsible for a whole business unit, guiding overall strategy by coordinating the efforts of brand managers and assistant brand managers and ensuring that the brand teams remain focused on the key strategic issues. It is your job to communicate with the executive wing and to ensure that your brands receive the resources and capital they need to grow.

Because you are responsible for the business unit's P&L, the workload can be heavy at times, but your generous compensation package justifies the effort.

Job Outlook

According to the 2004 Occupational Outlook Handbook from the U.S. Bureau of Labor Statistics (BLS), employment in the field of marketing overall is expected to increase faster than average—at a 21 to 35 percent clip—through 2012. The BLS says that this sustained job growth will be supported by increasingly intense domestic and global competition in consumer products and services, but cautions that budding marketers should expect increased competition for full-time corporate marketing positions as marketing projects (including brand management) are increasingly outsourced to ad agencies and contract specialists. Corporations seem to be maintaining their wait-and-see attitude toward new marketing hires as they monitor the still-tentative economic recovery.

Brand managers who managed to hang onto their jobs through the recession have been forced to work with drastically reduced budgets, leaving them hard-pressed to deliver the major product wins they need to advance their companies—and careers. On the other hand, brand managers with specialized scientific or industry expertise may find they are in a stronger position to land plum positions with major ad agencies as the economy begins to show signs of life.

Additional Resources

BrandChannel.com (www.brandchannel.com)

BrandWeek.com (www.brandweek.com)

MarketingPower.com (www.marketingpower.com)

Business Development

Career Overview

Business development (also known as biz dev) is exactly what it sounds like: It involves figuring out how to build or develop a business. You can find business development jobs in all industries—at everything from tech start-ups to huge pharmaceutical companies. What the work entails depends on how established a company is and what its business model is.

Business development people constantly ask: "What ten things will have the biggest positive impact on my company's business, and how can we make them happen?" Their objective is to expand the market reach or revenue of their companies in ways that make the most of their companies' resources and capabilities.

Biz dev executes company strategy by "doing deals" with complementary businesses. Exactly what that means varies from company to company. A deal might be a co-branding initiative, a technology- or content-licensing arrangement, an e-commerce partnership, or some combination of the three.

Business development involves varying degrees of sales and strategy. In some companies, biz dev people may focus on getting new corporate sales accounts, while in others they may lead new product development. At larger companies such as Time Warner, Cisco, or Microsoft, one of biz dev's many responsibilities may be to decide which smaller companies the company should acquire next to ensure that it retains its market strength in the future.

Working in business development is an excellent way to become adept at business strategy while gaining hands-on experience in negotiating deals and managing partner relationships. Business development jobs are also highly cross-functional, requiring close collaboration with various internal and partner-company teams such as sales, engineering, and marketing to ensure that a deal is consummated. With its focus on strategy, biz dev steers the direction of a company—the deals forged today determine what the rest of the company will be working on tomorrow.

Requirements

If you're interested in business but don't want to go the traditional route of working for a consulting or investment-banking firm, biz dev may be a good alternative. The best way to get into business development is by first gaining experience in finance, consulting, or corporate sales. The minimum degree requirement for an entry-level position in business development is a BA or BS. For more senior positions, an MBA is often preferred, along with 5 or more years of previous business development or sales experience.

Business development positions at high-tech companies may require a technical background, or sales experience in a related field. Strategic-planning or corporate-development positions usually require a minimum of two years' experience in investment banking or consulting.

Networking with friends or alumni will give you an advantage getting your foot in the door. If you're asked in for an interview, be ready to demonstrate your knowledge of the company's business and show that you're familiar with its competitive landscape. Be sure to play up any experience you have in closing deals or managing relationships. And remember that recruiters will be seeking a keen eye for detail, solid communication skills, and analytical ability.

Career Tracks

In order of increasing sophistication, the three overlapping layers within business development are sales, partnerships, and strategic planning. Most biz dev jobs blend all three, although one area may be emphasized.

Sales

At some companies, business development might be better described as business-to-business sales. In many cases, the business development team and the sales team are one and the same.

Cold calling or prospecting for potential clients, members, or partners is often a task that falls to entry-level biz dev employees. These employees often have to hone their own "sales pitch" to convince other companies that a partnership would add value to their businesses.

As in traditional sales jobs, there's often an account-management aspect to business development—coordinating a variety of partner relationships and deal types, each at a different stage.

Partnerships

Companies of all sizes in all industries are building their businesses around partnerships—and it is business development's responsibility to initiate and manage such relationships.

Often the biggest challenge facing business developers is negotiating the terms of partnership deals. Getting another company interested in a partnership is just the beginning—drafting a contract and negotiating its terms is a process that can drag on for months.

Once both parties sign the contract, business development must work with other teams in a company (e.g., product management, marketing, and operations) to oversee the successful meeting of the terms of the partnership.

Strategic Planning

Some business development jobs aren't called that at all. Instead, they're called "strategic planning," or sometimes "corporate development." Strategic-planning jobs are found mostly at large, established companies seeking to expand and diversify their business. Just like management consultants, strategic planners spend a lot of time thinking about top-level strategy issues such as what new business activities their company should pursue, how it should position itself and market those activities, and which technologies it should invest in.

At some companies, strategic planning may be carried out by the corporate finance department. In such cases, biz dev jobs may resemble investment-banking functions such as mergers and acquisitions. For instance, if a company wants to acquire a new business unit, strategic planning may analyze the market to find a suitable business to acquire, determine an appropriate asking price for the company, and follow through the negotiation process.

If the acquisition takes place, strategic planning may help integrate the two companies. This task may be as simple as processing a stack of paperwork or as complex as relocating and reorganizing the activities and personnel of the two companies.

Strategic planning may also involve institutional investment—that is, parceling out the company's money to fund outside start-ups. In this way, strategic planning can be a bit like working in the venture capital industry. For instance, when high-tech companies invest in high-tech start-ups, strategic planners may perform due diligence on potential partners, determine how much to invest in a particular venture, and negotiate a stake in a company.

Job Outlook

In the long term, business development opportunities should grow, especially in growing industries such as pharmaceuticals and biotech, the Internet, and technology. The growth in business development careers is being driven by a variety of factors. For one thing, businesses are doing more and more on the Web, meaning there are more and more opportunities for alliances, partnerships, and other business activities between and among companies doing business on the Web, Internet companies, and Internet services companies. At the same time, the world economy is becoming increasingly globalized, meaning there's growing need for biz dev types to seek out and close business deals in new markets.

Recently, though, job seekers looking for biz dev positions have found themselves in an extremely tight market. These positions are not core to most companies' continuing operations, so during periods of cutting costs and hunkering down to just stay afloat until the economy recovers, most companies prefer to lay off biz dev folks rather than hiring them. Look for the situation to improve as the economy does, though.

Those with an aptitude for landing and structuring deals—lawyers, for instance, or investment bankers—have the best shot at landing plum business development jobs.

Additional Resources

JustSell.com (www.justsell.com)

McKinsey Quarterly: Alliances
(www.mckinseyquarterly.com/category_editor.asp?L2=25)

McKinsey Quarterly: Strategy
(www.mckinseyquarterly.com/category_editor.asp?L2=21)

National Association of Sales Professionals (www.nasp.com)

Technology Business Development Forum (www.ibdf.org)

Consulting

Career Overview

In the world of business, management consultants are jacks-of-all-trades. Working through consulting firms or as independent contractors, they advise corporations and other organizations regarding an infinite array of issues related to business strategy—from reengineering to e-commerce, change management to systems integration. From billion-dollar mergers and acquisitions to corporate reorganizations in which thousands of jobs are at stake, they are the directors behind the scenes of nearly every major event in the marketplace.

A career in consulting can encompass a wide variety of industries. Pretty much anybody with a specialty in a field can offer consulting service; to keep this profile specific, we've focused on management consulting, a broad category in its own right.

Most management consultants hold salaried positions at firms that cater to a clientele of mostly large corporations. They are assigned on a project basis to their firm's clients, who are billed by the hour for their services. Depending on the client's needs and the firm's functional specialty (or core competency, as it's often called), consultants conduct objective research and analysis on behalf of their client, and make recommendations based on their findings. Ultimately, management consultants take on the responsibility of improving their clients' businesses by affecting change through their recommendations.

Research and analysis are the main tools of the trade for management consultants. They analyze a business problem from various angles by conducting research, and forming and testing hypotheses. Research may consist of collecting raw data from internal sources—such as the client's computers or through interviewing the client's employees—and external sources, such as trade associations or government agencies. A consultant gets some of his or her most valuable data through surveys and market studies that they devise and implement themselves. The data must then be analyzed in relation to the client's organization, operations, customers, and competitors to locate potential areas for improvement and form solutions. These solutions are then recommended to the client and—hopefully—implemented. (Sometimes convincing a client to accept a consultant's recommendations can be the most difficult aspect of the job, and there is always a chance that the client may choose not to accept the consultant's recommendation at all.)

For those who enjoy problem solving and thinking about business strategy, consulting can be a very fulfilling career as well as an excellent jumping-off point for a management career or a future as an entrepreneur. On the flip side, frequent travel and long hours can make a consultant's schedule very demanding.

While consulting is great for people who like variety in their work, it is not for those allergic to structure and hierarchy. The large and elite firms tend to have a culture that mirrors that of their corporate clients, complete with a steep career-ladder: Only a select few make it to partner-level, and that's with an MBA and 6 to 8 years at the firm.

Requirements

Although the competition at top firms is intense, the qualities that recruiters look for are similar across the board. Besides outstanding academic records, firms want people who are problem solvers, creative thinkers, good communicators, and who have a keen understanding of and interest in business.

Top candidates will also have previous experience in the business world (consulting internships are impressive but not required) as well as a record of extracurricular achievement. Firms specializing in IT consulting or e-business may require technical skills and experience.

The recruiting process at the elite strategy firms and the Big Five-affiliated consulting firms is standard for undergraduates and MBAs at top schools, and begins on campuses in the fall. For those who are not in school (or not at one of the handful of schools where firms recruit), the recruiting process begins at the firms' websites, many of which offer online applications. Alternatively, interested candidates can mail their resumes and cover letters to firms directly or to the attention of the recruiting director at his or her preferred office location.

Candidates with experience in industry are much sought after, particularly by firms that have industry practices that correspond to candidates' backgrounds. Several firms hold specialized information sessions for experienced candidates as well as PhDs and JDs. Consult firms' websites directly or contact firms' human resources departments or local graduate schools for schedules and eligibility.

Recruiting at most consulting firms, particularly those with a heavy strategy orientation, is bound to include at least one case interview in which the candidate is asked to solve a made-up business problem. The interview is designed to test the candidate's problem-solving skills, understanding of basic business principles, and communication skills. While there's no one correct answer to most case questions, there are several tried-and-true approaches to solving them that recruiters look for. To learn more about case questions and how to crack them, get WetFeet's bestselling *Ace Your Case!* Insider Guide series.

Most firms offer internships to highly qualified undergraduates and those enrolled in MBA programs. Competition for internships can be even more intense than for permanent positions, but a successful internship can dramatically increase a candidate's chances of getting an offer after graduation. Recruiting for internships generally begins on college campuses in the fall. For more information, consult firms' websites.

Career Tracks

Consulting firms hire MBAs and other postgraduates right out of school or from industry. Most new MBA hires will come into a firm as associates; after 2 or 3 years they'll move to the next level, where they'll manage case teams. After managing projects for a couple of years, consultants may be promoted to principal, whereupon the focus shifts to more intensive client work and the selling of services. Finally, after 6 to 8 years with a firm, a consultant might be promoted to partner. The benefits of partnership are big increases in salary and responsibility. The key function of partners at most firms is to cultivate clients and sell them new business.

Additional Resources

Consulting Central (www.consultingcentral.com)

Dowjones.com (www.dowjones.com)

Corporate Finance

Career Overview

If you work in private enterprise, your company measures its success at the end of the year by comparing how much money it made to how much it spent. If it has made more than it has spent, it was a good year. If it has made less than it has spent, it was a bad year—or the company is in an investment phase. (In other words, like Amazon.com, it spent more than it made because the company and its investors believed it would realize a profit in the near future.)

People who work in corporate finance and accounting are responsible for managing the money—forecasting where it will come from, knowing where it is, and helping managers decide how to spend it in ways that will ensure the greatest return.

This career profile focuses on opportunities in corporate finance and accounting in private industry.

Accounting concerns itself with day-to-day operations. Accountants balance the books, track expenses and revenue, execute payroll, and pay the bills. They also compile all the financial data needed to issue a company's financial statements in accordance with government regulations.

Finance pros analyze revenue and expenses to ensure effective use of capital. They also advise businesses about project costs, make capital investments, and structure deals to help companies grow.

In spite of their different roles, finance and accounting are joined at the hip: The higher levels of accounting (budgeting and analysis) blend in with financial functions (analysis and projections). Thus, finance and accounting are often treated as one, with different divisions undertaking particular tasks such as cash management or taxes.

Requirements

Finance and accounting jobs require critical, detail-oriented thinking. If you have a knack for using numbers to understand patterns that influence business, you're going to be valuable to a company. If you can't crunch and analyze them, this isn't going to be the right job for you. You should also like, and be good at, solving problems and be able to think critically about the numbers you're working with.

Finally, if you can effectively evaluate business scenarios and recommend a course of action based on quantitative research, finance may be just the career for you. Internships are always a great way to strengthen your resume and differentiate yourself from other candidates. An MBA will make you attractive to companies hiring for budgeting, planning, and strategy functions.

Many firms hire outstanding undergraduates and MBAs for training programs: some are finance and accounting specific, and others rotate trainees throughout the company. If you have your heart set on corporate finance and analysis, do a knockout job during that particular rotation and develop a good relationship with your manager.

If there is no formal program, you'll have to make the most of on-the-job training, so try to find a position that will expose you to a variety of projects. Find out what the career path in corporate finance is at your company and cultivate a mentor. A mentor can explain what projects will round out your background and what courses you can take to prepare yourself for a higher level assignment. You can also check out job listings on the Web to see what kind of experience and certification the jobs you're interested in require.

If you want to pursue a lifelong career as a number-cruncher, you'll probably have to knuckle down and get an advanced degree or certification—a CPA, MBA, or CFA could all come into play—at least to work in the more senior budgeting, planning, and strategy functions. You'll also need to keep track of the regulatory changes that affect how information is reported.

There are other ways in: Experience with an investment-banking firm can lead to a financial-analysis position for a specific business line or to a corporate-development position if you have several years of experience. At the higher accounting tiers, one of the most straightforward routes to becoming a controller (a supervisory accounting role) is to start working for one of the large accounting or auditing firms and then go into corporate finance.

Career Tracks

Although conditions vary at different companies, people going into corporate finance generally start their careers either as staff accountants (for the corporate-reporting function) or as financial analysts (for a business group or function). In both roles, you'll supply management with the information it needs to make smart, opportune decisions.

Staff accountants consolidate information for the official corporate financial reports—primarily comparing the present to the past. Financial analysts, on the other hand, are assigned to either a product line or business unit. They help management set up profit objectives, analyze current unit results, and anticipate future financial performance. Over time, financial analysts and staff accountants eventually specialize in one of the areas described below.

General Accounting

General accountants are responsible for producing all of the financial records a corporation uses to track its progress internally and to meet government regulations. Such workers also gather all the information needed to compute a company's balance sheet, profit and loss statements, and income statements. They also track the corporate budget, cash flow, and pay all the bills.

Usually, your first job in general accounting will be in accounts payable or accounts receivable. Success in accounting might lead you to a position as a controller, overseeing a larger group, aggregating information, or working on portions of the corporate budget.

Internal Audit

When most people think of an audit, they think of an outside audit—a large accounting firm like Ernst & Young checking the corporate books on behalf of the shareholders. However, most large companies have an internal-audit group that regularly visits individual company branches and checks the company's accounting systems.

Internal auditors perform the investigative and corrective work that ensures the external auditors don't find anything. The internal-audit group reviews the quality of the data, making sure it's both accurate and complete. Internal auditors also evaluate whether the corporate-accounting procedures are effective and universally followed. Finally, internal auditors introduce or revise procedures to improve efficiency and reduce costs.

Divisional Financial Services

In this area, you work with each division's business team to prepare financial plans, make forecasts, and compare actual financial results to forecasts. You may also evaluate the financial consequences of alternative strategies.

Responsibilities include everything from analyzing new business opportunities to restructuring a business or developing a capital-spending program. The primary concerns are to find better ways of using company assets, reduce costs, and research ways to develop better forecasts. Financial services evaluates the risks versus potential return of any course of action and develops recommendations so that managers can pick the most profitable strategies, depending on their goals.

Taxes

Activities in this area involve administering taxes (i.e., paying taxes on time—or finding loopholes to avoid paying them) and planning how to decrease the company's tax burden. Responsibilities include working with attorneys on tax litigation, researching tax laws and reporting requirements by nation (if the company is international), and keeping up with new government rules and regulations.

Large companies have an entire department dedicated to recommending methods to minimize the tax impact of any business decision such as a new division launch, a capital-spending plan, or purchasing a new company. Investments and pensions also need to be managed with an eye toward minimizing taxes. The tax department helps structure transactions, makes recommendations on the timing of acquisitions or sales based on what else will be written off that year, and can decide what corporate-reporting structure reduces taxes—for example, creating a wholly owned subsidiary versus having an internal division.

Treasury

The treasury department is responsible for all of a company's financing and investing activities. This department works with investment bankers who help the corporation raise capital with stock or bond sales or expand through mergers and acquisitions. Treasury also manages the pension fund and the corporation's investments in other companies. The department also handles risk management, making sure that the right steps are taken to safeguard corporate assets by using insurance policies or currency hedges.

Cash Management

This is a company's piggy bank. The cash-management group makes sure the company has enough cash on hand to meet its daily needs. The group also sees to it that any excess cash is invested overnight by picking the best short-term investment options. And it negotiates with local banks to get regional business units the banking services they need at the best price.

Corporate Development and Strategic Planning

Corporate development involves both corporate finance and business development. Finance experts in corporate development study acquisition targets, investment options, and licensing deals. Often they assess the best firms to buy or invest in, such as pre-IPO cutting-edge technology companies with complementary products that could either extend the company's product line or mitigate a potential future competitor. Corporate development jobs require planning and analysis know-how and the kind of skills that investment bankers working merger-and-acquisition deals put to use.

Job Outlook

In the shorter term, the outlook for folks in corporate finance and in-house accounting is getting brighter; after several years during which corporate hiring was quite slow, the economy shows signs of picking up, which means more corporate spending, more mergers and acquisitions, and so on—and more work for corporate finance types.

Longer term, as economies continue to intermingle globally, opportunities for sophisticated financial analysis and planning should grow. If the technology industry is any indication, companies will increasingly complete their own mergers and acquisitions in-house, creating more opportunities for people in finance who are able to think strategically. This means a greater demand for people with higher degrees who can develop more theoretical financial models, develop currency hedges, or estimate another company's future earnings and current value.

As more and more accounting functions become automated by software, those accountants and financial analysts able to do analytical work and think strategically will have much better prospects than those who stick to keeping the books. Graduate degrees, extensive analytical experience, and good regulatory knowledge will help keep you employed over the long term.

Additional Resources

CFO.com (www.cfo.com)

Investors' Business Daily (www.investors.com)

Institutional Investor Online (www.institutionalinvestor.com)

Knowledge @ Wharton: Finance and Investment
(knowledge.wharton.upenn.edu/category.cfm?catid=1)

McKinsey Quarterly: Financial Services
(www.mckinseyquarterly.com/category_editor.asp?L2=10)

Ohio State University List of Finance Site
(www.cob.ohio-state.edu/fin/journal/jofsites.htm)

General Management

Career Overview

General managers (GMs), also known as executives, or the executive team, run a company's business. They include the chief executive officer (CEO), chief operating officer (COO), president, and others. Their knowledge about an industry and their ability to provide direction can mean the difference between an organization's success and failure. They are involved in planning and policy making at almost every level, including both the long-term strategy and its day-to-day execution.

A GM decides what products to produce, which markets to go after, and the company's general philosophy. GMs are also expected to raise money, keep a company profitable, and answer to shareholders.

GMs also need to be their companies' biggest advocates. They communicate the value of their organizations to the outside world. Employees, strategic partners, shareholders, and even a company's chairperson rely on the general management team to promote the company's interests at every turn. GMs give their subordinates a reason to want to work for them. They instill a sense of pride in shareholders.

General managers tell the press why people should care about their products, marketing strategy, and goals. Without their guidance a company could flounder. General managers bring a measure of order and purpose to their organizations.

Small businesses and start-ups often have limited management teams. The founders, who take on the titles of CEO and president, typically lead such companies. As a company grows and departmentalizes, the general management function is divided into a family of positions.

While the CEO and president remain committed to the overall mission of the organization, other positions have more specialized responsibilities. Some examples are the chief operations officer (COO), chief financial officer (CFO), chief technical officer (CTO), and general manager (GM). Underneath them are department heads who run specific areas of an organization, such as marketing or human resources. They in turn hire and oversee managers who handle the day-to-day supervision of lower-level employees.

In this way, larger corporations have developed a well-defined chain of command. Lower-level employees answer to operational managers, who oversee their daily work. Many firms have several layers of frontline and middle managers. Such supervisors are responsible for managing the functions of an organization. They set project goals, make hiring decisions, settle staff disputes, and ensure that deadlines are met.

Operational managers report to department heads who set policy and determine the goals of their divisions. Department heads answer to the executive officer who controls their area of specialty. For example, the heads of Web development and information technology answer to the CTO.

Executive officers work together to set the goals and policies of a corporation. Their work is overseen by the general manager or president, who supervises the entire organization. Above them is the CEO, the highest-ranking manager. The CEO is held accountable for all aspects of the business. However, the CEO still has to answer to the board of directors.

In publicly held corporations, the board is ultimately responsible for the success of an organization. Members of the board have a fiduciary responsibility to look after the stockholders' (owners') interests first and foremost. If the company begins to falter, they have the right and the duty to correct the situation using any means possible, up to and including firing the CEO or any other top executive. In some cases, the board takes control of all managerial functions until a business has stabilized.

GMs can be found in every industry and organization, from publicly held companies to nonprofits and governmental agencies. Before entering management, GMs should have first proven themselves in their core industries. Usually they work for a while as operations managers, then slowly work their way up the corporate ladder.

Requirements

GMs must have significant experience in both industry and management. Quite a few have consulting experience at a top-tier strategy firm. An MBA or other advanced degree from an Ivy League or top-ten school can improve your chances of being offered a GM position.

Successful general managers have a lot in common. They are inevitably charismatic leaders who inspire their employees to reach their highest potential. They have developed strong written and oral communication skills, a flair for public speaking, the ability to make others feel at ease, and a strong, focused sense of purpose. Furthermore, they know how to get things done and aren't afraid to rock the boat to do so.

Long hours and extended travel are expected. Many GMs are on the road more than 90 percent of the time, visiting national and international offices, attending meetings and conferences sponsored by associations, monitoring operations, meeting with customers, and attending trade shows.

Career Tracks

The responsibilities of those in general management vary depending on the size and type of the organization involved. Smaller companies and start-ups usually have a few key GMs. As an organization grows and diversifies, general management duties will be broken up into a family of positions, which become increasingly specialized as the business grows larger. The following are descriptions of positions you can find in most publicly traded companies.

Chief Executive Officer (CEO)

A CEO is the highest-ranking manager in a company. Most are offered near-total autonomy in handling the day-to-day affairs of their organizations. All staff members work under their authority.

CEOs of publicly traded companies must answer to a board of directors. The board sets the standards by which a CEO must live. Board members can order a CEO's dismissal if they feel that he or she is not meeting the objectives they've set.

A CEO has to have a clear vision for the future of the company, then express that plan to employees, shareholders, and business partners, inspiring them all with confidence. CEOs must be able to raise money by getting venture capitalists to buy into their dreams, or Wall Street to underwrite a bond offering worth hundreds of millions of dollars. When necessary, CEOs will ruffle feathers. They know how to get things done and are willing to do whatever it takes.

Some CEOs are more involved in their companies than others. In small organizations, the CEO may be part of day-to-day operations. Other CEOs concentrate on promoting their companies by giving speeches, attending trade shows, cultivating the press, and acting as evangelists for their companies. They leave the direct management work to the president and general manager.

President

Working directly under the CEO, the president manages the daily operations of a company. While the CEO is the organization's superstar, the president works behind the scenes to make sure nothing gets bogged down in operations. He or she understands the corporate structure, how the industry is shaped, and what the primary objectives of the company are. The president interprets the vision expressed by the CEO and puts it into language that can be followed by everyone within the organization. Most of the president's time is spent working with other executive officers, particularly the COO. Together they ensure that the company's main goals are being achieved. The president's job is demanding and full of pressure. Those who succeed in it are often promoted to the CEO level.

Chief Operations Officer (COO)

The COO works directly under the president and CEO. His or her primary job responsibility is to oversee department heads and other key executives. Together they establish the operational policies for an organization. The COO makes sure everything runs smoothly. As needed, he or she provides reports on operational functions.

While the chief operations officer's role is crucial, it is not one that receives a lot of press. As long as operations go as expected, the COO is left to his or her own devices. Successful COOs can be promoted to president or CEO.

General Manager

General managers fill a role similar to that of the president and COO. Typically, GMs work for manufacturing companies and oversee their day-to-day operations. They spend most of their time in the office, working with department heads and other chief executives. Their primary function is to understand how their businesses operate and how to achieve or maintain their long-term economic viability. GMs analyze financial data and are responsible for producing profit and loss statements. They directly oversee the product development, operations, finance, sales, marketing, and purchasing departments. GMs answer directly to the president, or possibly the CEO, and are often first in line for such positions if they become available.

Most GMs are seasoned managers with strong financial backgrounds. They may have worked at various positions within their organizations. At the very least, potential applicants must have significant industry experience. As with any other executive position, general managers are expected to perform at all times. Any decline in profits can lead to their termination.

Chief Financial Officer (CFO)

The CFO is responsible for managing and analyzing all the financial resources of an organization. He or she works with the CEO and other chief executives to plan and implement strategies that will maintain the company's success. CFOs determine how much capital their companies need to have on hand to operate properly. They also reinvest corporate profits in safe but lucrative business opportunities. Some other possible responsibilities include raising capital, acquiring or merging with other businesses, taking a company public, and analyzing changing tax laws.

CFOs usually have extensive accounting and finance backgrounds. They are detail oriented and highly analytical. Possible promotion opportunities include becoming a COO, general manager, or president.

Chief Technology Officer (CTO)

CTOs develop an organization's short- and long-term information technology goals. A CTO must keep abreast of technological developments in his or her industry, develop technology-related product strategies, evaluate development options, establish strategic partnerships, negotiate licensing arrangements, and manage all intellectual property-related matters. A CTO works with a CFO and COO to determine which technologies meet the needs of employees without breaking a company's budget.

Besides having a strong technical background, the CTO must be an accomplished manager. The most important skill for CTOs is the ability to analyze changing technologies and predict how future advances will affect a company's business model.

Job Outlook

Thanks to layoffs, an uncertain economy, and a series of corporate scandals, general managers have been under intense pressure by their shareholders and the press. Across corporate America, these pressures have been compounded by the SEC's close scrutiny. Though many of these pressures remain in place, as the economy's prospects have improved so has the job security for general managers.

According to the Bureau of Labor Statistics, positions for general managers will grow at the same rate as jobs overall between now and 2010. Competition for general management positions is always competitive. The role is high profile and pays well, often with significant bonuses and stock ownership accompanying six-figure salaries. (At Fortune 500 companies, salaries often start at the seven-figure level). The best opportunities will go to managers who have proven track records for improving their company's efficiency and competitive edge. Beware, however, because managers who fail to perform are often let go after short tenures.

If you can manage to make your way to a general management position, you'll be in a comfortable place career-wise. High-level GMs receive many corporate perks, including spacious offices, administrative support, large severance packages, and subsidized worldwide travel. The hours can be long and pressure intense, but the financial incentives are commensurately rich.

Additional Resources

American Management Association (www.amanet.org/index.htm)

BRINT.com (www.brint.com)

ExecuNet (www.execunet.com)

McKinsey Quarterly: Organization
(www.mckinseyquarterly.com/category_editor.asp?L2=18)

McKinsey Quarterly: Strategy
(www.mckinseyquarterly.com/category_editor.asp?L2=21)

Investment Banking

Career Overview

The intensely competitive, action-oriented, profit-hungry world of investment banking can seem like a bigger-than-life place where deals are done and fortunes are made. In fact, it's a great place to learn the ins and outs of corporate finance and pick up analytical skills that will remain useful throughout your business career. But investment banking has a very steep learning curve, and chances are you'll start off in a job whose duties are more *Working Girl* than *Wall Street*.

Wall Street is filled with high-energy, hardworking young hotshots. Some are investment bankers who spend hours hunched behind computers, poring over financial statements and churning out spreadsheets by the pound. Others are traders who keep one eye on their Bloomberg screen, a phone over each ear, and a buyer or seller on hold every minute the market's in session. Traders work hand in hand with the institutional sales group, whose members hop from airport to airport trying to sell big institutions a piece of the new stock offering they have coming down the pipeline. Then there are the analytically minded research analysts, who read, write, live, and breathe whichever industry they follow, 24/7.

Investment banking isn't one specific service or function. It is an umbrella term for a range of activities: underwriting, selling, and trading securities (stocks and bonds); providing financial advisory services, such as mergers and acquisition advice; and managing assets. Investment banks offer these services to companies, governments, nonprofit institutions, and individuals.

Traditionally, commercial banks and investment banks performed completely distinct functions. When Joe on Main Street needed a loan to buy a car, he visited a commercial bank. When Sprint needed to raise cash to fund an acquisition or build its fiber-optic network, it called on its investment bank. Paychecks and lifestyles reflected this division too, with investment bankers reveling in their large bonuses and glamorous ways while commercial bankers worked nine-to-five and then went home to their families. Today, as the laws requiring the separation of investment and commercial banking are reformed, more and more firms are making sure they have a foot in both camps, thus blurring the lines and the cultures. The action and players are still centered in New York City and a few other money centers around the world, but the list of players is getting smaller as the industry consolidates. Today, leading banks include Merrill Lynch, Goldman Sachs, Morgan Stanley, Citigroup, Deutsche Bank, Credit Suisse First Boston, and J.P. Morgan Chase. These and other firms are regular visitors to campus career centers.

Investment bankers issue financial products; sell and trade them, invest in them, research them, and advise others on financial transactions. A full-service investment bank includes three major professional divisions: investment banking (which includes corporate finance, mergers and acquisitions, and public finance), sales and trading, and research.

Nearly all banks have a staff of research analysts who study economic trends and news, individual company stocks, and industry developments in order to provide proprietary investment advice to institutional clients and in-house groups, such as the sales and trading divisions. The research division also plays an important role in the underwriting process, both in wooing the client with its knowledge of the client's industry and in providing a link to the institutions that own the client's stock once it's publicly traded. However, in light of recent corporate scandals, in which banks were accused of favorably analyzing investment clients of the bank, there is growing pressure on Wall Street to separate its research and banking functions. This aspect of the industry could look quite different in the next several years.

The corporate finance group (frequently known as "banking" or "CorpFin") serves the sellers of securities. These may be either Fortune 1000 companies looking to raise cash to fund growth or, frequently, private companies wanting to go public (i.e., to sell stock on the public markets for the first time). Think of investment bankers as financial consultants to corporations. This is where CEOs and CFOs turn when they're trying to figure out how to finance their operations, how to structure their balance sheets, or how best to move ahead with plans to sell or acquire a company.

The activities of the CorpFin department can range from providing pure financial advice to leading a company through its first equity issue (or IPO). As a result, industry or product knowledge is key, and many investment banks divide their corporate finance departments into industry subgroups, such as technology, financial institutions, health care, communications, entertainment, utilities, and insurance, or into product groups like high-yield, private equity, and investment-grade debt.

The job of salespeople is to ensure their bank's financial stability by getting investors to commit to buying (subscribing to) stock and bond issues before the new securities actually hit the market. The mergers and acquisitions department provides advice to companies that are buying other companies, or which are being acquired by others.

Requirements

If you have an MBA or other advanced business certification, you'll be paid more for a position than someone with a fresh BA. But those with prior experience always get first shot, so be sure to get an internship. Industry expertise and prior corporate finance work can also be a way in, but you'll have to be patient.

Career Tracks

While the various groups within an investment bank support each other, the work and responsibilities in each group vary.

Corporate Finance

Investment bankers are like financial consultants for corporations—which is precisely where the Corporate Finance Group comes into play. As a member of Banking or CorpFin, you serve the sellers of securities—Fortune 1000 companies in need of cash to fund growth, and private companies that are looking to complete an IPO—by buying all the shares or all the bonds a company has for sale, which are then resold by your firm's sales force to investors on the market.

Many investment banks divide their corporate finance departments into industry subgroups, such as technology, financial institutions, health care, communications, entertainment, utilities, and insurance, or into product groups such as high-yield, private equity, and investment-grade debt.

As an investment banker in corporate finance, you will underwrite equity and debt (bond) offerings, help firms devise and implement financial strategies, analyze their financial needs (such as how to structure balance sheets and when and how to proceed with funding initiatives), and work with the sales and trading departments to determine valuations for new offerings.

Mergers and Acquisitions

The mergers and acquisitions group (known as M&A) provides advice to companies that are buying another company or are themselves being acquired. M&A work can seem very glamorous and high profile. At the same time, the work leading up to the headline-grabbing multibillion-dollar acquisition can involve a Herculean effort to crunch all the numbers, perform the necessary due diligence, and work out the complicated structure of the deal. As one insider puts it, "You have to really like spending time in front of your computer with Excel." Often, the M&A team will also work with a CorpFin industry group to arrange the appropriate financing for the transaction (usually a debt or equity offering). In many cases, all this may happen on a very tight timeline and under extreme secrecy. M&A is often a subgroup within corporate finance; but in some firms, it is a stand-alone department. M&A can be one of the most demanding groups to work for.

Public Finance

Public finance is similar to corporate finance except that instead of dealing with corporations, it works with public entities such as city and state governments and agencies, bridge and airport authorities, housing authorities, hospitals, and the like. Although the basic services (financial advisory and underwriting) and the financial tools (bonds and swaps, but no equity) are similar to those used for private-sector clients, numerous political and regulatory considerations must be assessed in the structuring of each deal. A particular key issue involves how to get and maintain tax-exempt status for the financial instruments the client will use.

Sales and traders sell and trade securities. Read the career profile on securities sales and trading for more on what they do.

Research

Research departments are generally divided into two main groups: fixed-income research and equity research. Both types of research can incorporate several different efforts, including quantitative research (corporate-financing strategies, specific product development, and pricing models), economic research (economic analysis and forecasts of U.S. and international economic trends, interest rates, and currency movement), and individual company research. It's important to understand that these are "sell-side" analysts (because they in effect "sell" or market stocks to investors), rather than the "buy-side" analysts who work for the institutional investors themselves.

As a researcher, you'll meet with company management and analyze a company's financial statements and operations, provide written and oral updates on market trends and company performance, attend or organize industry conferences, speak with the sales force, traders, and investment bankers about company or industry trends, develop proprietary pricing models for financial products, make presentations to clients on relevant market trends and economic data, offer forecasts and recommendations, and watch emerging companies.

Job Outlook

Undergrads and MBAs from top schools are recruited for a number of openings that's always been small but that, in the current environment of cost cutting, is now smaller than it's been in years. Competition is fierce, so if you're not from a top-tier school, you may need to be more resourceful and persistent. Networking is key so make use of your alumni connections. Though relatively few people come into the industry from other fields, it can be done, especially by those who have a technical background in a specific industry and an aptitude for and interest in finance. Otherwise, expect to start at the bottom.

Additional Resources

InvestorLinks.com (www.investorlinks.com)

SNL Financial (www.snl.com)

The Motley Fool (www.fool.com)

Wall Street Journal (online.wsj.com/public/us)

Marketing

Career Overview

When you think about cola, what do you think? Coke? Pepsi? That's due to marketing. What comes to mind when you think of computers? Dell? Apple? IBM? That's no coincidence. Those companies have spent a lot of money so that you'll associate a generic product such as a computer with a brand name.

Broadly speaking, marketing is the intermediary function between product development and sales. In a nutshell, it's the marketer's job to ensure that consumers look beyond price and functionality when they're weighing consumption options.

Marketers create, manage, and enhance brands. (A brand can be thought of as the way consumers perceive a particular company or its products and how a company reinforces or enhances those perceptions through its overall communications—its logo, advertising, packaging, etc.) Marketers want the consumer to ask: "Which brand helps me look and feel my best? Which brand can I trust?" Their goal is to make the brand they represent the obvious and uncontested answer to those questions in the consumer's mind. In marketing terms, this is called owning share of mind.

Of course, a brand can't be all things to all people. A key part of a marketer's job is to understand the needs, preferences, and constraints that define the target group of consumers (who may be from the same geographic region, income level, age range, lifestyle, or interest group) or the market niche corresponding to the brand. How can a company aggressively expand its market share and keep customers satisfied? That question is central to everything a marketer does.

Marketing is a function at every company in every industry. In the consumer products industry, marketing (called brand management) is the lead function. In other industries marketing may play a supporting role to another function. At a high-tech company, for instance, marketing may play a supporting role to research and development. And in advertising, market research, and public relations, a specialized marketing function is the industry.

Requirements

Marketing people come from many different academic backgrounds, but certain backgrounds will help more than others.

For advertising, a degree in advertising, communications, or graphic design may open the most doors.

If you're interested in getting into brand management or market research, an education that includes courses in business, economics, or statistics will serve you better than a liberal arts major will. A marketing career of any kind requires a sharp, analytical mind; strong oral and written communication skills; and a keen interest in business and consumer behavior.

The best way to get into marketing, regardless of what you've studied, is by taking an internship. Many PR firms, ad agencies, and high-tech and Internet companies offer marketing internships. Unless you're enrolled in an MBA program, internships are harder to come by at consumer-products companies.

The large consumer-products companies recruit at select schools, and the best way to get hired by one of them is through on-campus recruiting. For PR, advertising, and marketing positions in other industries, your best bet may be to network or to contact firms directly.

Career Tracks

Some companies define marketing positions broadly, encompassing everything from market research and strategy to advertising, promotions, and public relations. Other companies have large marketing departments, with marketers dedicated to one of these roles. And still other companies contract out many marketing functions to firms that specialize in advertising, public relations, and market research. What follows are descriptions of some common marketing roles.

Market Research

For a company to capture a market, it first must understand that market. Whether the intended target for the product is individual consumers or businesses, the company must know what motivates consumers, what their needs and purchasing habits are, and how they view themselves in relation to the rest of the world.

Market researchers use surveys, studies, and focus groups to collect data on a brand's target. Some companies have their own market-research divisions. Others hire specialized firms to conduct research for them. Ideally, market researchers should have both qualitative and quantitative analytical ability because their job depends on gathering data from human subjects, besides crunching numbers and interpreting the results.

Advertising

In broad terms, an advertising agency is a marketing consultant. It helps the client with all aspects of its marketing efforts—everything from strategy to concept to execution.

On the business side of advertising (as opposed to the creative or production sides), most jobs fall into account management, account planning, and media.

People in account management act as a liaison between the agency's various departments and the client. They manage the execution of ads by making sure ads are created within the allocated schedule and budget. Account planners focus on consumers, conducting research on the target demographic to get to know what motivates its behavior in the marketplace. In the media department, planners decide where to place ads, based on that demographic data, and buyers buy the ad space.

Promotions

Companies in which marketing is a particularly strong function may have a dedicated promotions staff to create programs that unite advertising to purchasing incentives such as coupons, special discounts, samples, gifts, rebates, or sweepstakes. To promote its promotions, the staff may use direct mail, telemarketing, advertisements, in-store displays, product endorsements, or special events.

Public Relations

Public relations personnel manage communications with the media, consumers, employees, investors, or the general public. They are the spokespeople for their own company or for client companies, if they work for a public relations firm. They may write press releases to promote new products or to inform the investment community of financial results, business partnerships, or other organizational news. If they're in media relations, they may respond to information requests from journalists, pitch stories to the media, or even ghostwrite op-ed pieces about the company.

In general, the goal of the public relations specialist is to portray the company in a flattering light, publicize its products and services, uphold its public image in a crisis, and generate positive buzz around its business and corporate practices.

Job Outlook

According to the 2002 to 2003 Occupational Outlook Handbook from the BLS, overall employment in the field of marketing is expected to increase faster than average—exhibiting a 21 to 35 percent growth—over the next decade. The BLS points to growing domestic and global competition in consumer products and services as a key reason for this job growth. However, these projections are based on data collected in 2000, and may be adjusted downward—due to the U.S. economic downturn since 2000—once data from 2001 to 2003 are available. The BLS also cautions that overall, there will be increased competition for the available opportunities in the field of marketing.

Additional Resources

BrandWeek (www.brandweek.com/brandweek/index.jsp)

Knowledge @ Wharton: Marketing
(knowledge.wharton.upenn.edu/category.cfm?catid=4)

MarketingPower.com (www.marketingpower.com)

McKinsey Quarterly: Marketing
(www.mckinseyquarterly.com/category_editor.asp?L2=16)

ProductScan Online (www.productscan.com)

Operations

Career Overview

The operations team creates the infrastructure of a company. Operations employees help determine where an organization should be based, its employment policies, accounting practices, distribution channels, and much more. While individual departments determine how corporate procedures are implemented, operations makes sure they are designed optimally in the first place.

The chief operations officer is a senior member in most organizations. The COO works with the CEO and company president to determine the company's vision. Their ideas are filtered down through the rest of the company.

Senior operations managers determine where an organization is based, what its facilities will look like, which vendors to use, and how the hiring policy will be implemented. Once the key decisions are made, lower-level operations personnel carry them out.

Accountants and controllers watch the books. Administrators and managers supervise line employees. Sales reps and customer service agents ensure clients get what they've paid for. If a problem exists, operations personnel will be the first to hear about it. They work to find a solution, and then set about fixing the problem.

While operations is a key component of any successful company, it is back-end work. Most support functions fall under operations' control. Such functions include customer service, logistics, production, maintenance, and administration. Sometimes, depending on the size and scope of an organization, operations will also include sales, accounting, programming, and marketing. The goal of the operations department is to find solutions to problems before they affect the bottom line.

Requirements

While you can get a customer service job with little experience, most operations positions require a 4-year degree and at least some industry background. Most universities offer degrees in operations management. But a degree in business, accounting, or administration is just as good. If you are interested in climbing the corporate ladder, you should consider getting an advanced degree.

Most VPs and COOs have an MBA, and many have a PhD. Without such degrees, promotions to higher levels will take a lot longer. It may also be more difficult to land a job at another organization.

To be promoted, an individual must prove he or she can be a good supervisor, get a job done right the first time, manage all aspects of a project, and keep it within budget parameters. A detail-oriented personality, strong analytical skills, and the ability to thrive in a team environment are necessities.

Career Tracks

The operations department is responsible for ensuring a company operates as efficiently and economically as possible. Exactly which functions it controls depends on the size and structure of the organization.

Controller

The controller watches out for the financial well-being of an organization. He or she manages the books, creates profit and loss statements, keeps projects within budget parameters, and prepares financial reports. Controllers work closely with operations managers and other accounting personnel. A strong financial background, an understanding of business processes, and a detail-oriented nature are prerequisites.

Facilities Coordinator

Facilities coordinators design the physical environment of an organization. The facilities coordinator is interested in how a building's design, layout, furniture, and other equipment affect the efficiency and profitability of the business that uses them.

The facilities coordinator will buy office furniture and supplies, determine when more space is needed, select appropriate vendors, and be responsible for the facilities budget. Besides having a business management background, the facilities coordinator needs to have a keen understanding of how working environments affect employee productivity.

Logistics Engineer

A business needs to plan how work orders will be distributed throughout its organization. The logistics engineer is the person primarily responsible for such planning. He or she is interested in improving the efficiency and accuracy of order fulfillment, and will map out the process from beginning to end, always on the lookout for possible improvements. This is a detail-oriented position that requires strong problem-solving skills and an in-depth analysis of business processes.

Project Manager

Most projects will have a single leader who watches over them from beginning to end. The essential role of the project manager is to establish group goals. He or she will also supervise the work of lower-level staff, ensure deadlines are met, put in requests for additional supplies and staff, and keep a particular project on time and under budget. In most cases, the project manager will answer to the operations manager.

Operations Analyst

An operations analyst analyzes how the current operations infrastructure is working. He or she attempts to find areas where the system breaks down and then finds ways to improve it. Strategies may include changing the work environment, changing employment policies, using different vendors, or changing the process. There is a great deal of administrative work involved. This position answers to the operations manager.

Operations Manager/Director

The operations manager or director watches over his or her department, the size and scope of which depends on the organization involved. A large company may have several operations managers. Their job is to determine how the processes in their departments should be implemented and what duties need to be performed.

An operations manager also hires and manages lower-level staff, selects the vendors, completes departmental financial analyses, and determines the budget. The operations manager reports to the VP of operations or chief operating officer.

Chief Operations Officer (COO)

One of the senior managers in any business organization, the chief operations officer is responsible for making sure that the entire back end of an organization operates as efficiently as possible. (The general management career profile has more about senior management roles.) The chief operations officer could be responsible for marketing, programming, customer support, sales, accounting, distribution, legal, or just about any other business function you could think of.

While the CEO is supposed to be the visionary for a company, the COO is a company's administrator. Without his or her involvement, a company could fail. The COO is a seasoned professional with many years' experience. He or she reports to a company's CEO and board of directors.

Job Outlook

The Bureau of Labor Statistics predicts that the number operations positions will grow at the same rate as the average for all occupations between now and 2010. Recent downsizings have made the job market competitive, with many more qualified applicants than positions currently available. But with tightening belts comes the need for quality management to ensure business is running efficiently—which is increasing demand for facilities and operations managers. There is also a move to save costs by consolidating operations roles, so being flexible and willing to take on expanded responsibilities will give you a leg up on the competition. As the economy improves, look for opportunities in this area to grow.

Additional Resources

BRINT.com (www.brint.com)

McKinsey Quarterly: Operations
(www.mckinseyquarterly.com/category_editor.asp?L2=1)

McKinsey Quarterly: Organization
(www.mckinseyquarterly.com/category_editor.asp?L2=18)

Project Management

Career Overview

Project management is an art, a skill, and a demanding full-time job. Project managers (PMs) are key employees in such industries as construction, engineering, architecture, manufacturing, and real estate development, but many opportunities for PMs exist outside these areas. In computer hardware and software for example, project managers are responsible for launching new products, developing new technologies, and managing alliance programs with strategic partners.

Large corporations such as insurance companies and banks may also hire PMs to manage the implementation of new standards or practices in their many branch offices. Internet companies often look for project managers to oversee site launches or the development of new applications.

Whether a project involves constructing a building, releasing a product, or launching a rocket, project managers make sure everything comes together in a timely, cost-effective manner—and take the heat if it doesn't. Their high-profile, high-risk work demands multitasking ability, analytical thinking, and excellent communication skills.

Project managers live and breathe by their schedules. In most cases, a project is planned down to the daily or even hourly level, and a formal schedule is developed using the critical path method (CPM), a precedence-based technique that determines the sequence in which things must happen. Milestones punctuate most project schedules, indicating the required completion of various steps.

Resource allocation is another big part of a project manager's job. If you are running a software development project, for example, you have to know how many engineers will be available and how many hours they'll need to work. Likewise, if you're running a construction project involving cranes and excavators that must be leased on an hourly basis, you'll need to know when to have those machines on site to get the most work done for the least money. Balancing limited labor, materials, and other resources is a difficult task that earns a good project manager top dollar.

Requirements

Educational requirements for project managers vary greatly according to the type of projects they manage. For construction projects, a civil engineering degree is usually required. High-tech PMs may need a degree in electrical engineering or computer science. In all cases, the most successful project managers have some type of formal business training, such as an MBA. Project management has a direct effect on a company's bottom line, so a PM must be able to evaluate a project's financial repercussions from a corporate point of view.

Project managers also need strong leadership skills, the ability to set and stick to a schedule, multitasking ability, analytical thinking, strong communication skills, and an orientation toward getting things done.

Professional certification in project management is available through the Project Management Institute, which bestows the profession's most globally recognized and respected credential—certification as a Project Management Professional. To obtain the PMP credential, applicants must satisfy requirements involving education and experience, agree to a code of ethics, and pass the PMP certification examination. Many corporations require PMP certification for employment or advancement.

Career Tracks

Project Manager

In this position, you may run a project yourself or lead a management team, delegating task management to assistants. PMs report to the "owner" of a project—whether that's a real estate developer, a government agency, or your company's senior management. You're not paying the money, but you take responsibility for the project's proper completion.

Senior Project Manager

Many large organizations that tackle multiple projects at once (especially construction and engineering companies) employ a senior project manager. The senior project manager supervises a company's various project managers, coordinating the allocation of company resources, approving costs, and deciding which projects should take priority.

Job Outlook

As might be expected, project management opportunities depend on the number of projects taking place. When the economy is booming, demand for PMs is usually high. When the economy is slow, look for opportunities in hot industry sectors, where a lot of projects are taking place. A wide range of industries use PMs to handle everything from launching new products to leading restructuring efforts to converting MIS systems.

The Bureau of Labor Statistics predicts job growth for project managers in construction to increase about as fast as average for all occupations through 2010. Increasing complexity of construction projects could, however, drive demand slightly above average.

Additional Resources

Project Manager (www.projectmanager.com)

Project Management Forum (www.pmforum.org)

ProjectManagement.com (www.projectmanagement.com)

Securities Sales and Trading

Career Overview

Securities sales and trading is where the rubber meets the road in the investment banking industry. An investment bank relies on its sales department to sell bonds or shares of stock in companies it underwrites. Investors who want to buy or sell a certain stock or bond will place an order with a broker or sales representative, who writes the ticket for the order. The trader makes the trade.

Securities sales and trading are high-profile, high-pressure roles in the investment banking industry. Unlike other I-banking careers, such as corporate finance, public finance, and M&A, where the emphasis is on the team, securities salespeople and traders are independent, working on commission to bring to market the financial products that others create.

In the United States, the securities business revolves around markets (also known as "exchanges") such as the New York Stock Exchange, the Chicago Board of Trade, and Nasdaq, where debt, futures, options, stocks, and other financial instruments are bought and sold. Salespeople and traders are independent agents working under a simple contract: The firm provides a place to do business in return for a percentage of the business that salespeople and traders generate.

Salespeople are called brokers or dealers. As one of them, you're expected to build a "book" of clients. No matter how long you've been working, and no matter how many clients you have, you're expected to cold call. New brokers make as many as 600 cold calls a day. Most of the work takes place over the telephone: soliciting clients or selling a particular stock or bond issue. You'll use analyst research and every sales trick in the book to push your securities to investors.

Traders make money by trading securities. Although they're the ones who transact trades for the brokers and their clients, traders are primarily responsible for taking a position in a security issue, and buying or selling large amounts of stocks or bonds using an employer's (or their own) capital. When they bet right, they win big; when they bet wrong, they lose big.

Brokers and traders build their lives around market hours. On the West Coast, you'll start working before 6:00 a.m., so that you're ready to go when the opening bell rings. There's no flextime, no long coffee breaks, and no time to run errands.

Requirements

There are no hard and fast educational or professional prerequisites for selling securities. However, the National Association of Securities Dealers (NASD) and the Securities and Exchange Commission (SEC) require brokers to get licenses, depending on a particular broker's role:

- You'll need to pass the Series 7 General Security Sales License Exam to sell most types of securities.
- Individuals who wish to sell commodities or futures contracts must pass the Series 3 Exam.
- Most brokers also need to pass a Series 63 License Exam, dealing with state laws regarding securities sales.
- Managers need the Series 8 License for general sales supervisors in order to manage branch activities.
- Managers supervising options sales personnel or compliance need to pass the Series 4 License Exam.

Would-be salespeople must also pass a background check to make sure they have no criminal history that would preclude them from being an "honest" broker.

Aside from the background and license checks, branch managers hire salespeople based on evaluations of candidates' ability to think on their feet, communicate effectively, deal with numbers, and, above all, make cold calls. Traders can break in by assisting other traders on the floor and starting trading accounts.

Image means a great deal in sales and trading: How you dress, how you carry yourself, and how you act will be as impressive to a securities sales manager as your educational or professional background. If you have experience in sales, that's a plus, but a manager is really looking for people who will put in the hours, make the calls, and generate revenue. And as in all areas of financial services, networking is key. Scour your alma mater's alumni connections, pester your friends and relatives, and follow any lead that might get your foot in the door.

Career Tracks

In securities sales and trading, you're in business for yourself. If you are a sales representative, your career track will consist of building your business, or book, to the point where you have a substantial number of clients for whom you trade. If you're a trader, your career track will consist of trading financial instruments (stocks, bonds, and other securities).

As with securities sales, the job of the trader doesn't change over time; traders get sharper, develop better instincts, and benefit from experience as they go along. Due to the pressure of the career, few last to middle age.

If you're interested in trading, check out internship opportunities. Many firms offer summer positions to outstanding students, providing candidates with much-needed experience and connections. Check out a company's website to research its internship offerings.

Securities Sales Representative (Broker)

Securities sales representatives—or brokers—act as intermediaries between buyers and sellers, and they make money off of commissions. In some cases, such as when trading stocks, bonds, and options, they need to be registered as agents of an investment house. Brokers give advice to customers and then make deals happen. Usually they specialize in a particular type of security, such as futures, options, or bonds.

Those who do well make a lot of money and may get a larger office and an assistant, but the work remains fundamentally the same. Brokers are sometimes called dealers, investment advisers, investment counselors, or investment representatives, but the work is the same.

Branch Manager

Senior sales representatives who have proven themselves on the trading floor may become branch managers. Branch managers hire salespeople, fire those who don't do well, and make sure that brokers meet sales and revenue targets. While branch managers make additional income in the form of commission overrides (a percentage of the commissions made by the brokers working under them), they're responsible not just for their sales, but their office totals.

Floor Trader

Floor traders run around the floor of an exchange (e.g., the NYSE), swapping tickets and making trades. Floor traders are responsible for locating the buyers and connecting them with the sellers (or connecting the sellers with the buyers). As prices change quickly in a turbulent market, traders are under constant pressure to get deals executed at the prices their clients (or their employers) specify. If a trader can't find somebody to buy or sell at a specified price, the buy or sell order won't go through, and nobody profits: not the buyer, not the seller, and not the trader (or the trader's employer), because there's no commission. Traders work during an exchange's hours of operation, usually without breaks.

Desk Trader

Nasdaq is what might be called a "virtual" stock exchange, as there is no physical building where traders meet to make deals with each other. Brokers have a "Nasdaq desk," which means they can trade on Nasdaq. That desk is actually a bank of traders, all staring intently at their computer screens to see how the market is shaping up, speaking into several phones at once in a mad rush to find buyers or sellers whom brokers or online investors have requested. (Trades made through an online account, such as at Charles Schwab or TD Waterhouse, go directly to the trader, bypassing the broker.)

Job Outlook

With the early-2000s bursting of the tech bubble, the decline of the stock market, worldwide recession, and widespread distrust of corporate officers resulting from scandals at Arthur Andersen, Tyco, Enron, and other companies, the action in the markets pulled way back from the levels seen in the 1990s. As a result, salespeople and traders experienced a period of mass layoffs as investment banks and brokerages cut costs and consolidated.

As of early 2004, though, things are looking a lot better for folks interested in these careers—mainly because money's been pouring into the markets for the past year. Longer term, the picture looks bright as well: According to the Bureau of Labor Statistics, jobs in securities, commodities, and financial services sales should grow by 20 percent between 2000 and 2010, faster than the rate of job growth overall.

With online and self-service brokerages, investors can self-direct their own investment strategy, but most are willing to pay qualified professionals to guide them. No matter who actually places a buy or sell order, there will always be a need for securities traders who work behind the scenes, locating the buyers or sellers who are willing to accept the securities transactions their clients or brokers want to make. But expect to face rigorous competition for securities sales agent positions, where only the most experienced applicants will get the job.

Additional Resources

Investors' Business Daily (www.investors.com)

Institutional Investor Online (www.institutionalinvestor.com)

Knowledge @ Wharton: Finance and Investment
(knowledge.wharton.upenn.edu/category.cfm?catid=1)

McKinsey Quarterly: Financial Services
(www.mckinseyquarterly.com/category_editor.asp?L2=10)

National Association of Securities Dealers (www.nasd.com)

Ohio State University List of Finance Sites
(www.cob.ohio-state.edu/fin/journal/jofsites.htm)

Supply Chain Management

Career Profile

Supply chain managers attempt to integrate and optimize all the steps required to produce the right amount of the right product and deliver it to the end user at the right time. In other words, supply chain management (SCM) is involved in every aspect of getting products to customers, from raw materials to consumption. As an insider defines it, "Supply chain management is interested in everything that happens to a product from cradle to grave."

The focus of this profile is on those industries for which supply chain management is essential to remain competitive in the marketplace: manufacturing, retailing, and logistics and distribution. Manufacturing companies typically emphasize materials management and sourcing functions. Roles within the retail and merchandising industries tend to emphasize logistics, warehousing, and inventory management. Like retailers, the roles of logistics firms emphasize (what else?) logistics, inventory management, and warehousing. Most larger firms offer the entire range of logistics services from transportation and carrier services to warehousing and inventory management.

Job descriptions in supply chain management suffer from a blurring of responsibilities over titles, a lack of standard nomenclature for positions, and, often, a lack of distinction between ranks. In the first case, as perhaps is fitting for a discipline that is nothing if not interdisciplinary, the job description of a role may encompass a number of disciplines. For instance, in a manufacturing firm, a procurement or purchasing role might include inventory management responsibilities; in a distribution or logistics firm, a transportation role might include those inventory management responsibilities.

Requirements

In general SCM recruiters are not looking for generalists, even at the undergraduate level. Most firms and organizations have a select group of programs from which they recruit, and those programs, such as Arizona State and the University of Wisconsin at Madison, tend to offer degrees in supply chain management. If you aren't in a school at which the firm recruits, an internship might get you in the back door. Because the market is soft now, firms are demanding industry and functional experience even for entry-level positions. In the MBA world, firms look for supply chain coursework or dedicated supply chain programs.

Certifications aren't required, but they do help in a slack market. Common certificates are Certified Purchasing Manager (CPM) and CPIM (Certification in Production and Inventory Management). Nearly one quarter of purchasing professionals hold a CPM certification, and nearly 10 percent hold a CPIM certificate.

Clearly, proficiency in an enterprise resource planning (ERP) software package such as SAP, Oracle, or i2 greatly enhances your marketability. Detail orientation is always a prerequisite for supply chain jobs—you can't overdo attention to detail when communicating with prospective employers, either in informal conversations or during the interview process. Finally, because of the cross-functional nature of the field, communication and people skills are paramount.

Career Tracks

While there is no single career trajectory in supply chain management, most insiders we spoke with agree that the apex of the supply chain cosmos is vice president of supply chain management. The path has yet to be blazed for supply chain managers who attain the ranks of COO, let alone CEO. In the past, this has been due to the fact that logistics positions have been very specialized roles.

More recently, supply chain has been a cross-functional role and has yet to gain traction as a set career path in most corporations.

The good and bad news is that supply chain roles are highly specialized. Not only is it somewhat difficult to cross over mildly different functional roles, but functional knowledge doesn't transfer completely across industries. This means that one can't easily hop from one industry to the next—for instance, as a supply chain manager for Wal-Mart to one for BMW. While this means it is difficult to easily transfer across functions, it also means that there are fewer candidates nipping at your heels ready to take your job.

Having said that, here are a few of the general career tracks one can follow in supply chain management:

Supply Chain Manager

The supply chain manager role is the holy grail of supply chain management and logistics, both sought after and somewhat rare. The scarcity of pure supply chain manager roles comes from the fact that the role is interdisciplinary—a role that spans logistics and distribution, purchasing, manufacturing, inventory management, and even marketing and product development.

The supply chain manager reviews existing procedures and examines opportunities to streamline production, purchasing, warehousing, distribution, and financial forecasting to meet a company's needs. A supply chain manager typically develops strategies to cut costs, improve quality, and improve customer satisfaction.

Vice President, Supply Chain Management

At the top of the supply chain management food chain, the vice president is part of the senior management team and usually reports to the chief operating officer of a company. The vice president's purview often includes all supply chain functions, including logistics, facilities, and purchasing. The vice president translates executive strategies into supply chain functions. Reporting to the vice president, often, are directors of the various functional areas in supply chain.

Logistics Analyst/Manager

Analysts and managers work on a wide range of logistics functions, including warehouse and distribution operations, forecasting, planning, logistics information systems, customer service, and purchasing. Analyst roles might deal with an area within the logistics function, while senior roles such as manager or director roles involve overseeing a team of analysts. Managers negotiate and contract with suppliers and carriers, develop supply chain metrics and strategy, and oversee day-to-day management of logistics functions. Analysts devote much of their days to problem solving, forecasting, and ensuring that operations are running within determined metrics.

The ladder to a manager level position might take 5 to 7 years to climb, a director level or higher position 10 to 15 years.

Process Engineer

Process engineers typically analyze processes within any number of industries—manufacturing, distribution and transportation, or retail—and develop improved processes that make better, safer use of labor, materials, energy, and other resources. For instance, a process engineer in a distribution center might work to improve outbound and inbound traffic processes or invoice handling. In a manufacturing environment he might develop a better method for handling raw materials. Additionally, he might develop the metrics used to manage the processes once improved.

Supply Chain Consultant

The consultant is a senior role, usually post-MBA, that, along with the analyst and project manager, makes up the team on a consulting engagement. The supply chain consultant is a rare and desirable role in the field of supply chain management. The SCM consultant reviews existing procedures and examines opportunities to streamline production, purchasing, warehousing, distribution, and financial forecasting to meet a company's needs. An SCM consultant typically develops strategies to cut costs, improve quality, and improve customer satisfaction.

Job Outlook

With the economy seemingly picking up and real salary increases in 2003, the outlook for supply chain management in 2004 and 2005 looks healthy. However, most companies look for candidates with coursework in supply chain management or prior industry and functional experience in the case of midcareer job seekers. These qualifications limit the number of qualified applicants for the field and perhaps explain the relative salubriousness of the discipline.

While no role clearly outshines the others in terms of employer demand, more and more companies are reorganizing around supply chain management (as opposed to logistics or materials) and so supply chain manager roles are becoming more prevalent.

No single industry has the best outlook in 2004 and 2005. Instead, look for high-growth opportunities in burgeoning subsectors such as specialty pharmaceuticals and medical device manufacturing.

Additional Resources

Institute for Supply Management (www.ism.ws)

Supply-Chain Council (www.supply-chain.org)

JOB SEARCH GUIDES

Getting Your Ideal Internship

Job Hunting A to Z: Landing the Job You Want

Killer Consulting Resumes

Killer Investment Banking Resumes

Killer Resumes & Cover Letters

Negotiating Your Salary & Perks

Networking Works!

INTERVIEW GUIDES

Ace Your Case: Consulting Interviews

Ace Your Case II: 15 More Consulting Cases

Ace Your Case III: Practice Makes Perfect

Ace Your Case IV: The Latest & Greatest

Ace Your Case V: Even More Practice Cases

Ace Your Interview!

Beat the Street: Investment Banking Interviews

Beat the Street II: Investment Banking Interview Practice Guide

CAREER & INDUSTRY GUIDES

Careers in Accounting

Careers in Advertising & Public Relations

Careers in Asset Management & Retail Brokerage

Careers in Biotech & Pharmaceuticals

Careers in Brand Management

Careers in Consumer Products

Careers in Entertainment & Sports

Careers in Human Resources

Careers in Information Technology

Careers in Investment Banking

Careers in Management Consulting
Careers in Manufacturing
Careers in Marketing & Market Research
Careers in Nonprofits & Government
Careers in Real Estate
Careers in Supply Chain Management
Careers in Venture Capital
Consulting for PhDs, Doctors & Lawyers
Industries & Careers for MBAs
Industries & Careers for Undergraduates

COMPANY GUIDES

Accenture
Bain & Company
Boston Consulting Group
Booz Allen Hamilton
Citigroup's Corporate & Investment Bank
Credit Suisse First Boston
Deloitte Consulting
Goldman Sachs Group
J.P. Morgan Chase & Company
Lehman Brothers
McKinsey & Company
Merrill Lynch
Morgan Stanley
25 Top Consulting Firms
Top 20 Biotechnology & Pharmaceuticals Firms
Top 25 Financial Services Firm